BREAK, BREAK

a Legion Cycle play

Erin Lerch

BROADWAY PLAY PUBLISHING INC
New York
www.broadwayplaypublishing.com
info@broadwayplaypublishing.com

BREAK, BREAK

First edition: May 2024
I S B N: 979-8-88856-014-3

Book design: Marie Donovan
Page make-up: Adobe InDesign
Typeface: Palatino

BREAK, BREAK received its world premiere production with Legion Theatre Project and Artists' Theater of Boston in September, 2023. The cast and creative contributors were:

RACHEL..Melissa deJesus
MIRANDA ....Jordan Palmer
CLARK..Steve Auger
RED ....Michael J Blunt
GWEN..Chris Everett

Director..Josh Glenn-Kayden
Co-Producer..Anneke Reich
Stage Manager..Ames Lehrmitt
Assistant Stage Manager..Melee Lee
Scenic design..Ben Lieberson
Lighting design..Andrea Sala
Sound design..Anna Drummond
Costume design..Erica Desautels
SFX Mentor..Lynn Wilcott
SFX..Becca Cottrell
Prop design..Kelly Smith
Dramaturgy..Alison Yueming Qu
Fight/intimacy consulting..Alex M Jacobs

AUTHOR'S NOTE

BREAK, BREAK takes place shortly into the future of the continental United States, as an alien Legion arrives and devastates human civilization.

This play is one work within the Legion Cycle, which consists of multiple plays and audio dramas that all live in the same post-alien-apocalypse universe, but also each work as a standalone story. The Legion plays are intentional acts of rebellion within the American theatre. Where most sci-fi stories for the stage focus solely on the human characters, the Legion plays have traditionally featured multiple alien species onstage at once. There are always numerous queer and trans actors in roles that are about more than just being queer or trans. Legion stories have used the presence of nonhuman characters to investigate who has the privilege of being treated as a person, and who is seen as an outsider.

I thought this play would follow the two previous plays in that regard, featuring multiple alien characters and a wide scope. It didn't quite turn out that way—as I worked through the revision process, I discovered instead that this play was about isolation, and grief, and the importance of rebuilding connection and community after a traumatic event. In other words: oops, I wrote a Covid play by way of an alien invasion. But at the end of the day (and the end of the play), optimism and hope prevails. I needed that reminder that sometimes, there is a light at the end of the tunnel—you just have to choose to look for it.

A few things to keep in mind that myself and collaborators have discovered while working on plays and stories in the Legion world, to give you a starting place:

Keep in mind that this play is set in our world, in our future. The characters are as aware of science fiction stories as we are now, and they are aware that they're living through one of those stories.

Pace is incredibly important in this play. Every moment is precious. There should be no pauses where they are not noted, and if in the rehearsal room you find that it makes more sense to run through pauses that *are* noted, go right ahead. Earn the silences. Make sure they're pushing the action forward.

CHARACTERS & SETTING

RACHEL, *a radio DJ. Mostly bark, very little bite, at least at the beginning. Mid-late 20s, woman, she/her pronouns.*

MIRANDA, RACHEL'S *college friend. Former aspiring DJ herself, now happily otherwise employed. On the cynical side, practical (perhaps to a fault). Mid-late 20s, transfemme, she/they pronouns.*

CLARK, *co-founder, owner, and begrudging manager at the station. Was once the engineer, now training the new blood to keep it going. Stubborn, puts on a grumpy front. 60s, man, he/him pronouns.*

RED, *in training as the engineer. Very into the tech, not so into the people. A human of few words. 20s, nonbinary, they/them pronouns.*

GWEN, *a stranger, stranded. Just wants to get home. 30s-50s, she/her pronouns.*

Voices (pre-recorded):

CALLERS *(5), people calling in to the radio station. Named in the text, should each be different voices.*

KA2YO, *often goes by just "Yankee". Local ham hobbyist. Strong prepper and conspiracist tendencies. They/them.*

NJ3JEN, *goes by "Juliets." Local ham hobbyist. Newer to the hobby. She/her.*

EMERGENCY BROADCAST, *announcement from the military. Could even be computer generated.*

WARNING, *recorded voice. Southern accent would be great, if possible.*

KV5EDF, *goes by "Fox(Trot)". Ham hobbyist. He/him.*

Casting note: Trans and nonbinary roles in this play must be played by trans/nonbinary actors. That said, actors need not necessarily use the exact same pronouns as the characters—I would encourage trans and nonbinary actors to read for any parts that they feel are appropriate. I also encourage those casting this play to think expansively about the characters who may initially read as cisgender. Unless a character is specified as cis, the role is open to anyone who feels their identity aligns with the character's.

While the characters have not been written with a specific race in mind, under no circumstances should this play have an all-white cast. As you are making casting decisions, I encourage who you're centering and who we lose (and when). Consider if your casting choices are playing into harmful dynamics that already exist.

A radio station in Cranberry Township, Pennsylvania, about twenty miles north of Pittsburgh.

Time: The near future.

TEXT NOTES

A / indicates where the next line should interrupt the current line.

A line break in a character's text indicates a new thought.

Scene 1

(Darkness. Perhaps a radio jingle plays. Then we hear voices—first one, then more, growing gradually into a cacophony. It should be hard to pick out specific phrases, but some things come through clearly: "object approximately 20km in radius spotted just beyond the orbit of Saturn"; "moving under its own power—some kind of artificial object"; "government has announced a press conference tomorrow morning"; "calls to NASA contacts for further comment have gone unanswered"; and, from many voices, "aliens". As the noise reaches a peak, we hear RACHEL*'s voice cutting through.)*

(As RACHEL *speaks, lights up on the radio station broadcast room. The room is cramped—clearly not meant for more than a couple of people at a time—with a desk in the middle of the room. The desk is covered with equipment: several monitors, a sound mixing board, and a mic on a boom arm. An assortment of extra materials is boxed on shelves around the room, with a small second table tucked into one corner.* RACHEL *sits at the mic.* MIRANDA *sits at a second chair, listening as she taps away at her phone.)*

RACHEL: Goooood evening, western Pennsylvania. It's just turned eight o'clock, and you're listening to 103.7 WCRP. It's been one heck of a day, huh? For my regular night owls who might just now be tuning in for your nightly dose of Rachel, I've been going—oh, about eight hours straight now. Welcome to the party! Normally this is about the time where I'd be giving you the prompt for tonight's weirdo phone conversations, but today's about as far from normal as I think we're maybe ever gonna get. And given the past few years, that's saying something. So: let's talk about the aliens in the room. What do you all think about them? Do they come in peace? What do they want? Is it even real? The phone lines are open—give us a call and let's talk about it, right after a couple of tunes to get us in the mood. *(She clicks a few times on the computer, then mutes and leans away from the mic.)* Any luck?

MIRANDA: Nope.

RACHEL: Want to go outside, try calling again? I know the service is bad in here.

MIRANDA: Why? So they can tell me that "due to an overload of calls, your expected wait time is eighteen hours"?

RACHEL: Eighteen hours, seriously?

MIRANDA: And the apps are no better—I've checked them all. All flights suspended until God knows when.

RACHEL: Damn. Is Jess doing alright?

MIRANDA: For a certain definition of "all right". We're texting. They're on hold with two airlines at once.

RACHEL: I hope they get through.

MIRANDA: Me, too. *(A pause)* You sound good.

RACHEL: Hmm?

MIRANDA: On the mic. Good energy.

RACHEL: Thanks.

MIRANDA: I don't know if I'd be able to keep it together. What with all the…

RACHEL: Aliens.

MIRANDA: Right.
Fuck.

RACHEL: *(In agreement)* Fuck.

MIRANDA: I mean.

RACHEL: Yeah.

(Pause. Then, the door opens quietly, and CLARK *peeks into the room.)*

RACHEL: You're clear.

CLARK: You left the on-air light on.

RACHEL: Oops.

(She flips a switch nearby.)

CLARK: S'pose I shouldn't give you a hard time about it, given everything.

RACHEL: Not feeling up to the usual lecture today?

CLARK: Seems a little…trivial. In the grand scheme of things.

*(*CLARK *backs out of view, then a moment later, enters carrying an armful of ham radio gear.* RED *follows, carrying another box of gear. They both set the boxes down on the table in the corner.* RED *crawls under the desk to start plugging things in.)*

RACHEL: Jesus. What's all that?

CLARK: *(To* MIRANDA*)* And who, exactly, are you?

RACHEL: This is Miranda. My friend, visiting from out of town for the weekend, remember?

CLARK: Ah. Right. California.

MIRANDA: You have something against California?

CLARK: Had a bit of a bad time there back in the day. No offense meant.

MIRANDA: None taken, I think?

CLARK: Long way to come just for the weekend.

MIRANDA: I had work stuff in Cleveland, figured I'd stop in while I was nearby-ish.

RACHEL: She was supposed to fly home this morning, but…

CLARK: But.
Just don't touch anything. The equipment in here can be a tad ornery.

RACHEL: The equipment isn't the only thing.

CLARK: What?

RACHEL: You didn't even introduce yourself before you started bossing her around.

CLARK: Ah, shit.
Sorry, uh—Miranda, right?

MIRANDA: Right.

CLARK: Clark.

(He holds out a hand, and they shake briefly.)

CLARK: And that's Red.

*(*RED *sticks their arm out from under the table long enough for a brief wave.)*

CLARK: It's just, we don't have a lot of spare equipment, so I can be a little protective.

MIRANDA: It's fine. I promise not to break anything.

RACHEL: I promise not to let her break anything.

MIRANDA: Hey.

CLARK: Good.

RACHEL: Still confused about all…whatever that is.

MIRANDA: Looks like a ham radio set up.

CLARK: You into the amateur scene?

MIRANDA: My mom. She taught me some. I've always wanted to get back into it, but haven't had the space or budget, to be honest.

CLARK: That's a shame. All you need's a corner by a window.

MIRANDA: I'm not sure my landlord would be into me mounting an antenna on the building.

CLARK: Better to ask forgiveness than permission.

MIRANDA: Easy for you to say.

(MIRANDA's phone buzzes.)

MIRANDA: Oh! Be right back.

CLARK: Rain check.

MIRANDA: Sure.

(MIRANDA exits. RED emerges from under the table to start on the equipment up top.)

RACHEL: *(Indicating the ham gear)* Still confused.

CLARK: I thought, given everything, it might be good to have a ham setup here as well as at the house.

RACHEL: For what?

CLARK: Just in case.

RACHEL: In case of *what*?

(CLARK pauses, then hands RED a coil of wire.)

CLARK: Could you run that out to the antenna outside? Make sure it's not going to trip anyone.

(RED glances between RACHEL and CLARK, then grudgingly exits.)

RACHEL: They're not a kid, you know.

CLARK: They're my kid. In every way that matters, anyway.

RACHEL: Still.

CLARK: You're probably right.

RACHEL: Seriously, though. What's with all this? The main equipment is working just fine, unless something blew a fuse in the last sixty seconds.

CLARK: That radio only sends. This one can send and receive.

RACHEL: Ahhh. That how you talk to all your weird friends?

CLARK: It is, as a matter of fact.

RACHEL: And you want to do that in this particular room all of a sudden because…?

*(*MIRANDA *re-enters.)*

RACHEL: Hey. Everything okay?

MIRANDA: Yeah. Well, no. But yeah.

RACHEL: Right.

MIRANDA: What were you talking about?

RACHEL: Why Clark decided to make this room even more cramped than it already is.

CLARK: I thought it might be good to have some kind of link to the outside.

RACHEL: *(Waggling her phone at him)* What, you mean like this?

CLARK: Never hurts to be redundant.

RACHEL: What's with you?

CLARK: I have a bad feeling, that's all.

RACHEL: About the…?

CLARK: Yeah. And I had this old rig lying around looking all lonely, and I figured, what's the harm, right?

RACHEL: Sure.

CLARK: Could be it's for nothing.

RACHEL: Hey. If it makes you feel like you're doing something, that's enough.

(MIRANDA *rolls her eyes.)*

CLARK: Sure.
You taking calls, Rachel?

RACHEL: Soon. Got about half a song left.

CLARK: Bet folks will have a lot to talk about.

RACHEL: Probably.

CLARK: Thanks for coming in early, by the way. Phil didn't give me a lot of notice.

RACHEL: No prob. Not like I have anywhere better to be.

MIRANDA: How's your mom doing?

RACHEL: Fine, I think. I texted her earlier and she seems okay.

MIRANDA: Tell her I say hi.

RACHEL: Will do.

CLARK: Y'know, if things do go wrong…you'd be welcome to hole up here.

RACHEL: Do you really think we're going to need to "hole up" somewhere?

CLARK: I don't really know what to think.

MIRANDA: It's a distinct possibility.

CLARK: I'm just saying. It's an open invitation. To both of you.

MIRANDA: Thanks.

RACHEL: Yeah.
Oh, uh. Song's about done.

CLARK: I'll get out of your hair. Go make sure Red didn't fall off the roof or something. *(He exits.)*

RACHEL: *(Into the mic)* Aaaand we're back, folks. I hope you enjoyed that little Bowie interlude—not exactly my usual fare, I know, but it seemed to fit the bill. We've got our first caller on the air—Max from Cecil, you're live. What do you want to talk about?

CALLER 1: *(Staticky—a bad connection)* Can you hear me okay?

RACHEL: A little fuzzy, but we hear you.

CALLER 1: Sorry, I'm at work tonight, but I wanted to make sure and call in.

RACHEL: We're glad you did. What do you think's going on with all this alien stuff?

CALLER 1: I really don't know. I figure people a lot smarter than me will deal with all that. And hopefully, if the aliens don't mean well... well. I'm not in the service anymore, but there're a lot of good people still in, and they're gonna have something to say about it if those aliens try to pick a fight.

RACHEL: I hope you're right.

CALLER 1: Anyway, that's not why I'm calling. I've been listening a few years now, ever since I started working nights, and just wanted to make sure I said thank you. It's been nice to have a little company all this time.

RACHEL: It's my pleasure.

CALLER 1: Gotta get back to work. Boss man doesn't pay me to stand around talking. You keep safe now.

RACHEL: You, too.
Alright—caller number two, Sam from Evans City, you're live on WCRP.

CALLER 2: Good evening.

RACHEL: What's on your mind?

CALLER 2: Well, I'm not sure how you're going to feel about this, but I was hoping I could pray with you.

RACHEL: *(Startled)* Pray?

CALLER 2: Yes. My church group met up tonight—we're all feeling a little uncertain, I think—and it helped me to pray with them all, so I thought... Would that be alright?

RACHEL: I. Uh.

*(*RACHEL *looks at* MIRANDA, *who shrugs helplessly.)*

RACHEL: Tell you what. I don't really know how this goes—it's not exactly my thing—but if you want to say a little something, I bet there are folks out there who'd appreciate it.

CALLER 2: That's what I hope. Sorry, I'm a little nervous.
Dear Lord, I'll keep this brief. I know you have a plan for all of us, even if sometimes we can't exactly see it. All I ask is that you give a little comfort to anyone who needs it tonight. Bless us all, and keep us safe. Amen. *(A brief pause)* Are you still there?

RACHEL: We're here. Thank you, that was lovely.

CALLER 2: I just hope—

(Silence. Maybe a hint of static)

RACHEL: Sam? You still there?
Sorry, folks. Looks like we're having technical difficulties with the lines. Let's play a few tunes, and hopefully we'll be back as soon as we can. *(She presses a couple of buttons.)* Fucking hell.

MIRANDA: Does that happen a lot?

RACHEL: The praying? No, that's a first.

MIRANDA: No, the line going out.

RACHEL: Yeah. Unfortunately. *(She goes to the door, yelling offstage.)* Red. Red!
Fuck's sake.

*(*RACHEL *exits.* MIRANDA *checks her phone, then scoots over to look at the screens curiously, careful to keep her hands clear of any buttons. A moment later,* RACHEL *returns, followed by* RED.*)*

RACHEL: —literally went out mid-sentence. I thought you said you'd fixed it.

RED: I did.

RACHEL: Apparently not.

(Ignoring her, RED *sits at the desk and starts troubleshooting.)*

MIRANDA: I see your taste in music hasn't improved much.

RACHEL: Bite me.

MIRANDA: Tempting.

*(*RACHEL *makes a face at her.* MIRANDA*'s phone buzzes.)*

MIRANDA: Be right back.

*(*MIRANDA *exits.* RACHEL *paces back and forth behind* RED.*)*

RACHEL: How long is this going to take? I only queued up a couple of songs.

RED: Longer if you keep talking.

*(*RACHEL *sighs. She reaches for her own phone. Frowns at the screen. Types for a bit)*

RED: There.

RACHEL: It's fixed?

RED: Should be.

*(*RED *relinquishes the chair to* RACHEL, *who peers at the screen.)*

RACHEL: Hang out for a sec and make sure?

*(*RED *shrugs, nods.)*

RACHEL: Mind hitting the on-air light?

*(*RED *raises an eyebrow at her.)*

RACHEL: I don't want Miri coming back in not knowing we're live.

*(*RED *looks pointedly at the button, which is within arms' reach of* RACHEL. *They sigh and press it.)*

RACHEL: 'Preciate it.
Allllright, folks, we're back after those technical difficulties. Looks like we lost Sam, but we've got another caller on the line from Pittsburgh—Paul, can you hear us alright?

CALLER 3: I can hear you.

RACHEL: What's on your mind?

CALLER 3: Well it seems obvious to me that this whole thing's a hoax.

RACHEL: How so?

*(*MIRANDA *re-enters, being very careful not to make noise with the door.* RED *eyes her, but doesn't object.)*

CALLER 3: Come *on*. Aliens? What, the viruses and the false flags weren't enough? This has got to be the most ridiculous, unbelievable thing they've come up with yet. They just want to take away—

*(*RED *leans over and hits a button on the keyboard, cutting off the call.* RACHEL *turns.)*

RACHEL: *(Mouthed)* What the fuck?

*(*RED *shrugs.)*

RACHEL: *(Aloud)* Paul? You still there?
Looks like calls just aren't meant to be this evening.
I can take a hint. We'll try again later, but for now,

we've got a couple of good tunes coming up for you, including a new single just released this week. This is 103.7, WCRP. *(She hits a button, leans back from the mic, eyes* RED.*)*

RED: *(Utterly insincere)* Oops.

RACHEL: I had it under control. We get shit like that all the time.

RED: Sure.

RACHEL: Clark's not gonna be happy about that. "Free speech", yadda yadda.

RED: He'll live.

RACHEL: You're lucky he likes you.

*(*RED *shrugs, leaves the room.)*

MIRANDA: What'd I miss?

RACHEL: Not much. Everything okay?

MIRANDA: Mm. Not really.

RACHEL: Yeah. I'm sorry.

MIRANDA: Yeah.

RACHEL: Well, it's just gonna be more of the same from here. If you wanna head out, get some shut-eye, call Jess again, feel free. *(Pause)* Miri?

MIRANDA: I'll stay, if it's all the same to you. I don't really want to be alone right now. Especially if I can't go home.

RACHEL: If you want... you can take my car. Try and drive back to San Jose.

MIRANDA: Really?

RACHEL: Yeah.

MIRANDA: I appreciate it. But... it's a long drive. And given the state of the roads, I don't think I'd get far.

RACHEL: You're probably right.

MIRANDA: I really do appreciate the offer, though.

RACHEL: Yeah, yeah.
If things do go to hell, this wouldn't be the worst place to bunker down.

MIRANDA: Hmm.

RACHEL: It's soundproof, underground, and has a door that locks.

MIRANDA: How far are we from Pittsburgh?

RACHEL: I dunno, twenty miles?

MIRANDA: Not bad.

RACHEL: Plus, if we learn anything, we can broadcast it out to people.

MIRANDA: You really think anyone's going to be listening to 103.7 WCRP if fucking aliens attack us?

RACHEL: Maybe! You don't know. Can't hurt, right?

MIRANDA: It might, if the aliens hear us.

RACHEL: You really think the aliens are going to be listening to 103.7 WCRP?

MIRANDA: Maybe. You don't know.
But you're right. There are worse places.

(Pause)

RACHEL: Wanna choose some of the tunes?

MIRANDA: God, yes.

RACHEL: Have a look.

*(*MIRANDA *moves to the computer and starts scrolling down the list of songs.* RACHEL *scoots back, watching them. Checks her phone. Deliberately puts it aside.)*

Scene 2

(The next morning. Radio voices, overlapping and chaotic. Interspersed among them, we hear bits of the 8AM speech: "...have demanded our complete and unconditional surrender", "do not intend to give up our hard-won freedoms to these invaders from another world", "find shelter". The rest of the voices include: "many cities and counties are setting up safehouses for those who want to bunker down", "attack is expected at 12PM sharp", "get underground if you can", "get out of city centers—they are targets".)

(Then: RACHEL *at the mic.* CLARK *is sitting in the corner tinkering with his ham setup quietly.)*

RACHEL: This is 103.7 WCRP. By my watch, it's just about 10AM, which means we have just a couple of hours left before... Well. It doesn't look like we're gonna be surrendering, so I suppose that's when sh—when uh, things will go down. If you haven't already, find a friend or two and a place to bunker down, ideally with no windows. All we need to do is stay alive. We've been sinking all our hard-earned taxes into the military for a long time, so let's sit back and let them actually do something for once. In the meantime, if you want to give us a call, the lines are always open.

*(*RACHEL *leans away, flicks the "on air" light off. Scrubs at her eyes. Checks her phone)*

RACHEL: Christ.

CLARK: What now?

RACHEL: My mom. She's stuck on the highway out of Cincinnati. She's worried the city will be a target.

CLARK: She might be right about that.

RACHEL: Yeah, maybe. Not sure being out on the open road is a better plan.

CLARK: Six rotten eggs one way, a half dozen broken the other.

RACHEL: I don't think that's a thing.

CLARK: It is now.
Any callers on the line?

RACHEL: Yeah, actually. One.

CLARK: Well, go on and answer it.

RACHEL: In the middle of a song?

CLARK: Why the hell not?

(After a moment, RACHEL *turns to the mic.)*

RACHEL: Sorry to interrupt anyone who was jamming out, but it looks like we have a caller! Alex from Pittsburgh, you're on the air.

CALLER 4: I don't know what else to do at this point.

RACHEL: What do you mean? Are you alright?

CALLER 4: Far from it. I'm hoping maybe there's someone listening who can help me. I've got four kids I need to get to the shelter outside of the city, and my car's completely dead. Won't even give me the no-battery light—it's just. And no one else seems to be picking up the phone right now. Uber and Lyft are both dead ends. Even 911 has a queue.

RACHEL: Jesus.

CALLER 4: Chances are we're just gonna get stuck in traffic, but I can't—I can't stay here. They say the cities are going to be targets, and my kids…

RACHEL: Where are you?

CALLER 4: Shadyside. Carron Street.

RACHEL: Okay, got it.
Looks like we've got another caller on the line—

hopefully they can help. Give us a call back if you need to, okay?

CALLER 4: Thanks.

RACHEL: Ray, you're on the air.

CALLER 5: I'm on my way. Might be a bit cramped, but we'll make do.

RACHEL: Glad to hear it.

CALLER 5: Gonna hang up now, just wanted to let your last caller know I was coming.

RACHEL: Thanks.
Looks like that's all the callers for now. We'll keep the lines open as long as we can. This is 103.7, WCRP.

(She mutes the mic, trades a glance with CLARK. *Before either can say anything,* MIRANDA *enters the room, a duffel bag over one arm, a large reusable tote bag under the other, and rolling a second suitcase behind her.)*

RACHEL: Cutting it a little close, aren't you?

MIRANDA: I had to ditch the car and walk the last mile.

RACHEL: Jesus.

MIRANDA: Gave me time to call Jess. They're getting the hell out of San Jose.

RACHEL: My mom, too.

MIRANDA: Good. Safer that way. Here.

(She drops the suitcase off by RACHEL, *finds an out-of-the-way spot for the duffel.)*

RACHEL: Thanks. Find everything okay?

MIRANDA: Yeah. Lucky I was packed to fly home. Hopefully I got everything you needed.

RACHEL: I'm sure it's fine. What's in there?

MIRANDA: Everything shelf stable that I could carry.

RACHEL: Good idea.

MIRANDA: *(To* CLARK*)* Do you have any buckets?

CLARK: Probably. Check the janitor closet—turn right out the door, second door down.

MIRANDA: Thanks.

RACHEL: What do you need buckets for?

MIRANDA: Water. In case the water lines go down.

RACHEL: Do you think that's going to happen?

MIRANDA: There are fucking aliens, Rachel. I have no idea what's going to happen. But better over-prepared than under.

RACHEL: Almost forgot about your prepper tendencies.

MIRANDA: They have the right idea about a few things. And very wrong ideas about others.

RACHEL: Fair enough. Need help?

MIRANDA: *(Indicating the mic)* Don't you need to…?

RACHEL: I've got at least an hour. If the FCC is even paying attention at this point. And if we're gonna bunker down, we should have everybody inside when—at noon.

MIRANDA: What about Red?

CLARK: Should be back soon, too.

MIRANDA: Come on, then.

*(*RACHEL *and* MIRANDA *exit.* CLARK *turns back to his ham setup, tuning the frequency.)*

CLARK: This is Whiskey Three Lima Echo Sierra. Got a new rig set up at the station. Anyone read?

*(*CLARK *waits. Static. He changes the frequency. Tries again)*

CLARK: This is Whiskey Three Lima Echo Sierra. Anyone read?

KA2YO: Kilo Alpha Two Yankee Oscar here. Shouldn't you be under cover, old man?

CLARK: I could say the same to you, Yankee.

KA2YO: Oh, I'm safe as houses. Moved my rig to a secure location ages ago.

CLARK: Good to hear.

KA2YO: Hey, maybe this'll give me time to finally get that damn repeater up and running.
Did you need something?

CLARK: Just checking to see if the old rig still worked.

KA2YO: Reading you loud and clear.

CLARK: Good.

*(*RED *enters quietly, carrying a bag of their own. They consider their options, then tuck it away in an already-cluttered corner of the room.)*

KA2YO: 73, Whiskey. Good luck today.

CLARK: You, too. Clear.

*(*RED *makes a noise while putting their bag away.* CLARK *jumps.)*

CLARK: Jesus. Don't do that.

RED: It's not on purpose.

CLARK: I know, I know. Sorry. Just a little tense today.

RED: Mmhm.

CLARK: Radio's working.

RED: Mm.

CLARK: Got everything you need?

RED: Mm. You need anything?

CLARK: My house is only five minutes from here.

RED: Plenty of time.

CLARK: I can always go later.

*(*RED *gives him a look.)*

CLARK: Alright. I'll make a list.

*(*RED *nods, satisfied. Checks the time)*

RED: Better make it quick.

CLARK: *(Checks as well)* …Right. *(He turns back to the table, pulling out a pad of paper.)*

Scene 3

(Evening of the same day. Radio voices, growing more and more panicked: "ships spreading out over the entire United States", "shadows over New York City, Los Angeles, Orlando…", "lost contact with our central office", "can see something glowing on the horizon to our east, right where the city is", "no survivors reported out of Atlanta", "casualty reports are staggering")

(Then: RACHEL *at the mic.* MIRANDA *sits nearby, fiddling with her phone aimlessly.* CLARK *is at the ham radio, now with a headset plugged in. More supplies have been piled against the walls—food, blankets, buckets of water.)*

RACHEL: This is 103.7, WCRP. The hour is, uh…just turned eight o'clock. We haven't been able to get cell service in a bit, and the wifi went down a few hours ago. Seems pretty safe to assume that was the aliens, trying to make it so we can't talk to each other. Good news is, it looks like our little radio tower hasn't caught their attention yet, and we'll keep broadcasting as long as we can. The local amateur radio network is still up and running—kind of—so we're still getting some news. If you have a ham radio, tune in and let us know how you're doing.

Folks…there's no easy way to say this. They dropped some kind of…they flattened Pittsburgh. From what we're hearing, there's nothing left standing within the city limits Everything from Summer Hill to Mount Oliver is nothing but rubble and ash. It's just gone. And we're not the only ones. It sounds like they've done the same to just about every major city. New York, Chicago, San Francisco, Atlanta, DC… If you're still out there to hear, be careful, okay? Keep your heads down and your chins up. Don't let them win.

*(*RACHEL *turns away from the mic. A moment)*

MIRANDA: "Keep your heads down and your chins up," huh?

RACHEL: I thought it was a nice turn of phrase.

MIRANDA: It's not bad. Not sure it's worth risking our necks over.

RACHEL: We went over this already. Someone has to—

MIRANDA: Get the word out. I remember. Just not sure why it has to be us.

(Pause. The low drone of an alien ship in the distance, growing louder. CLARK *pulls the headset off his head, listening.)*

MIRANDA: Shit.

RACHEL: What?

MIRANDA: My phone's dying.

RACHEL: So? Not like there's service.

MIRANDA: No, but.
I just wish I knew if they'd made it out. Jess.

RACHEL: Yeah. I hope they did.

(The drone is right overhead, thrumming the walls. Everyone tenses, bracing themselves until it starts to fade again.)

RACHEL: God*damn* those things are loud.

CLARK: Red's out there.

MIRANDA: Oh, shit.

RACHEL: Those things are huge. No way they'd see them from up there.

MIRANDA: You have no way to know that. They could see through walls for all we know.

(A knock on the door to the room, "shave and a haircut" style. Everyone jumps. CLARK *gets up—it is clearly not easy for him—and moves to the door, opening it to admit* RED.*)*

MIRANDA: Did it see you?

RED: *(Shaking their head)* Saw it first. Got inside.

MIRANDA: Thank fuck.

CLARK: How's it look out there?

RED: Same.

CLARK: Any movement?

*(*RED *shrugs, points to the ceiling, making a circling motion.)*

RED: Ships. Fliers.

CLARK: No people?

(A head shake)

MIRANDA: If there were, what exactly would we do about that?

RACHEL: Help, obviously.

CLARK: What she said.

MIRANDA: How? It's cramped enough in here as it is. And even we can't survive off of what we've managed to scrape together from your apartment and the break room.

RACHEL: We could make it work.

MIRANDA: For how long?

RACHEL: Until we kick those fuckers to the curb.

MIRANDA: You sound awfully sure about that.

RACHEL: You're not?

MIRANDA: No.

(Another ship goes by overhead, this one much faster. Everyone flinches.)

MIRANDA: We need to talk about what we're going to do long term.

CLARK: We can cross that bridge when we get to it.

MIRANDA: Pretty sure we've already crossed it.

RACHEL: Things are bad. No one's denying that.

MIRANDA: Just that things will stay bad, right?

RACHEL: Exactly. Could be the military swoops in tomorrow and drives them away.

*(*RED *makes a derisive sound.)*

MIRANDA: Even if they did, there's no going back. Pittsburgh is gone. San Jose is gone. Philly, Cleveland, Seattle, Chicago—every major city in the entire country is *gone,* and probably half the population along with them.

CLARK: Jesus.

MIRANDA: Even if the military pulls something amazing out of its collective ass and drives the aliens off tomorrow…there's no fixing this. Not for a long, long time.

RACHEL: So, what, we should just go running out and give ourselves up?

MIRANDA: No. But we can't stay here forever, either. We need to find other people—people with resources beyond a few bags of canned food.

RACHEL: It's an active warzone out there.

MIRANDA: I'm aware. I'm not saying leave right now, just—we need to be ready. Have a plan.

RACHEL: You and your fucking plans.

MIRANDA: I like to be prepared.

RACHEL: Were you prepared for this? A fucking alien invasion?

MIRANDA: That's not fair.

RACHEL: I can't—I can't have this conversation. Not yet. Okay?

MIRANDA: Rachel—

RACHEL: It's too soon. We have food, we have water, we have a safe place to hide. Can we just…see what happens.

CLARK: I agree with Rachel. There's too much we don't know about how this is going to go.

MIRANDA: We can't even be sure this place is safe. Especially if we keep broadcasting our location.

CLARK: We have a responsibility to get the word out.

MIRANDA: What word?

CLARK: Whatever we can learn. We're in a prime position here—we have lines to the outside for information, and a way to get that information out to others.

MIRANDA: What information? That they bombed Pittsburgh? I think everyone in a hundred mile radius heard that explosion.

RACHEL: But we know exactly how far out it reached, thanks to Bravo. And this isn't over yet—who knows what other information we might get.

MIRANDA: Is it worth putting all of us in danger over that?

RACHEL: Yes.

CLARK: We have a responsibility.

*(*RED *nods.)*

MIRANDA: Jesus. Fine. I guess let's just…wait and see.

RACHEL: *Thank* you.

MIRANDA: What do we do in the meantime?

CLARK: I think I've got a few old paperbacks kicking around somewhere in here.

MIRANDA: Great.

(The power suddenly flickers out, the room going black.)

RACHEL: Jesus—fuck.

MIRANDA: There goes the power grid.

RACHEL: Fuck.

MIRANDA: I was wondering why it hadn't gone yet.

CLARK: Just you wait.

MIRANDA: For what?

(The lights come back. Some of the equipment in the room—the essential stuff—hums back to life.)

CLARK: "We don't need solar panels," you said. "It's a waste of money," you said.

RACHEL: I didn't say that.

CLARK: Not you. *(He turns to* RED.*)* Huh? What do you say *now*, buckaroo?

RED: I didn't anticipate aliens.

(A pause. Then, RACHEL *starts laughing—the kind of helpless, exhausted laughter that you can't really control.* RED *looks surprised.)*

MIRANDA: Rachel? You okay?

*(*RACHEL *keeps laughing.)*

RED: Wasn't that funny.

CLARK: When was the last time she slept?

MIRANDA: At least twenty-four hours.

CLARK: That'd do it.

*(*RACHEL *finally gets it under control.)*

RACHEL: Sorry. Sorry, I just—

MIRANDA: You just need to get some rest.

RACHEL: No, I need to…the radio.

CLARK: Oh, please. What are they gonna do, fine us?

RACHEL: But—

RED: Sleep.

MIRANDA: You're no use to anyone if you're too punch-drunk to keep it together.

RACHEL: What if we hear something people need to know?

CLARK: Then I'll do the announcement. I was a DJ longer than you've been alive, before my lungs went to shit. Or your friend here—I'm sorry, remind me?

MIRANDA: Miranda.

CLARK: Right—Miranda. Or hell, even Red.

*(*RED *makes a face.)*

CLARK: We can handle it.

RACHEL: Okay, okay. *(She gets up, starts for the door. Pauses)* Oh. Right.

MIRANDA: Here.

*(*MIRANDA *piles up a few blankets in a corner.* RACHEL *watches, swaying a bit on her feet. When* MIRANDA *is done,* RACHEL *moves to the makeshift bed.)*

RACHEL: Wake me up if you need me.

MIRANDA: *(Not unkindly)* Go the fuck to sleep, Rachel.

*(*RACHEL *crawls into the bedding.)*

Scene 4

(A few days later. This time, the radio voices are fewer and more staticky. "Devastation across the entire country", "sporadic fighting continues along the coast", "ships and winged aliens patrolling the skies")

(Then: RACHEL, *at the mic.* CLARK *is listening at first from the ham station, but partway through the intro, he turns to the ham in response to hearing something.)*

RACHEL: You're listening to 103.7, WCRP. This morning marks five days since Pittsburgh fell, but we're living proof that there are still people hanging in there. Alien ships continue to fly over the area, so stay under cover as much as possible. Seems like it's every half hour at least. If you have a ham radio, or anything you can jury-rig, there's a few folks in the area doing their best to keep us updated. 145.26 MHz. If you don't, keep your regular old radio tuned to this frequency, and we'll keep you updated as long as we can. Chin up. We can make it through this.

(She turns away. Lights up on the rest of the stage. RED *is now sleeping in the blanket pile, face buried in their arms. Things have been unpacked from the bags—piles of dirty clothes in varying degrees of neatness, a couple of books, etc. A half-full garbage bag sits in the corner with food wrappers and the like.* MIRANDA *is digging through one of the bags of*

food, which is looking pretty empty by now. Their phone is plugged in to a wall outlet.)

RACHEL: *(To* CLARK*)* More news?

*(*CLARK *motions for her to hush, listening intently.)*

RACHEL: Guess that's a yes.

CLARK: Hush. *(A moment while he listens. To the radio.)* Thanks for the info, Juliets. 73. Whiskey Three Lima Echo Sierra clear.

*(*CLARK *removes his headset. A moment.)*

RACHEL: Clark?

CLARK: There are aliens in downtown Pittsburgh.

MIRANDA: What?

CLARK: Aliens. Walking around downtown—or what's left of downtown, anyway.

RACHEL: What kind?

MIRANDA: What *kind*?

RACHEL: What do they look like, I mean.

MIRANDA: Does that matter?

RACHEL: Kinda! I'd like to know how far away I'll see them coming, for one thing.

MIRANDA: …Fair.

CLARK: She didn't get a good look at them, but… human-ish in size, maybe a bit bigger. They're mostly moving in packs, she said. Digging bodies out of the rubble.

MIRANDA: Alive or dead?

CLARK: Both.

(A low, rumbling drone starts to build in the background.)

RACHEL: Is she okay? Like, is she safe?

CLARK: For now.

RACHEL: Can we do anything to help?

Doesn't sound like it. Just keeping her head down, like we are.

(The drone goes overhead. RED *sits up, rubbing their eyes and glaring at the ceiling.)*

RACHEL: I'll let folks know when I do the evening broadcast.

MIRANDA: If anyone's listening.

CLARK: Assuming they are, it's important to stick to a schedule. Otherwise…

RED: They'll think we're gone.

MIRANDA: …Right.

RACHEL: *(To* CLARK*)* Have you heard from anyone else?

CLARK: Not yet, today. Bravo usually checks in in the afternoon, and Yankee's a night owl, so we won't hear from them before six. If we hear from them at all.

RACHEL: Is it just the three left?

CLARK: …Yeah.

RACHEL: Damn.

MIRANDA: How many ham friends did you have?

CLARK: 'Friends' is a strong word, but in terms of people I talked to regularly…I dunno. Dozens.

MIRANDA: And now there are three.

RACHEL: That are still on the radio. The others might still be okay.

CLARK: Sure. Maybe.

MIRANDA: Or maybe the aliens are following the radio right to them.

RACHEL: Don't you think, if they were listening, they'd be here by now?

MIRANDA: Maybe. Or maybe they just haven't gotten to us yet.

*(*MIRANDA *comes up with four granola bars, passing one to* RACHEL.*)*

RACHEL: If I wasn't so hungry, I'd be getting sick of these by now.

MIRANDA: Well, I've got good news and terrible news for you, then.

*(*MIRANDA *goes to* CLARK, *setting the bar down next to him. He pats her hand absently, attention clearly on the radio.* RACHEL *takes a bite of her granola bar.)*

MIRANDA: Which do you want first?

RACHEL: Uh…good news, I guess.

MIRANDA: Good news. No more granola bars.

RACHEL: Okay, and…?

MIRANDA: Bad news. No more food.

(They nudge RED*'s shoulder, leaving the bar next to them.* RED *nods in thanks.)*

RACHEL: What?

MIRANDA: You heard me.

RACHEL: We can't be out of food already.

MIRANDA: We are. Or close enough to it. This isn't a fucking bomb shelter, Rachel. We're lucky it lasted this long.

RACHEL: Clark? Any secret stashes you might be hiding from us?

CLARK: Do you really think I'd do that?

RACHEL: No. I was… it was a joke.

RED: Not a very good one.

RACHEL: Sorry. Guess the humor well is running a little dry.

MIRANDA: That's the other thing we're out of.

RACHEL: Humor?

MIRANDA: Water. Whatever was left in the pipes is gone, and what we managed to save before they ran dry isn't much better.

RACHEL: Great.

MIRANDA: We need to start planning long term.

RACHEL: Not this again.

MIRANDA: Yes, this again.

RACHEL: Miranda—

MIRANDA: You wanted to wait. I waited. But it's been almost a week, and honestly, I don't see the situation changing anytime soon. Do you? Do any of you?

CLARK: No.

*(*RED *shakes their head.)*

RACHEL: You don't know that.

MIRANDA: What I know is that the military is on the defensive, and unless they have a hell of an ace up their sleeve, it doesn't seem like that's going to change.

RACHEL: So you're a military strategist now?

CLARK: She has a point.

MIRANDA: Thank you.

RACHEL: Fine. Worst case scenario. What's your plan?

MIRANDA: We can't stay here.

CLARK: Where else could we go?

MIRANDA: There's a military base just west of Philly.

RACHEL: Philly? That's gotta be hundreds of miles from here.

MIRANDA: Two-fifty. Ish.
I looked it up before the network went down. Took screenshots and everything.

RACHEL: That'd take days to walk.

MIRANDA: And?

RACHEL: You said we're out of food.

MIRANDA: Almost. If we stretch it, I think we could make it.

RED: Clark can't.

CLARK: My legs aren't what they used to be. My lungs, neither.

RACHEL: And we're not leaving you.

MIRANDA: One person could survive here a lot longer than four.

RACHEL: We're not leaving Clark here alone. Right, Red?

*(*RED *nods, then considers.)*

RED: Driving?

RACHEL: They'd see us. Right?

MIRANDA: Probably. It's a lot easier to spot a vehicle than a few people on foot.

CLARK: Agreed.

RACHEL: So.

MIRANDA: We don't have a lot of good options here.

RACHEL: Leaving him here alone isn't an option at all. I can't believe you're even considering it, Miri!

MIRANDA: I have to. We don't have the luxury of perfect options here—slow starvation one way, possible capture another.

(The drone of an alien ship in the distance.)

RED: What if we got more food?

MIRANDA: From where?

RACHEL: Clark—your contacts, they said the aliens are only in the city itself, right?

CLARK: That's—I mean, that's what they said, but it's not like it's a perfect system.

(The alien ship is overhead. They wait for it to begin to fade.)

RACHEL: Okay. Assuming the intel is good, they're not too far out of the city. They're probably not this far out yet.

MIRANDA: We don't know that for sure. They could be waiting for us outside.

RACHEL: Then it doesn't matter what we're leaving to do, they'll catch us either way.

MIRANDA: And if we lead them back here? At least if we're going somewhere else anyone who stays behind will be safe. Safer, anyway.

RACHEL: Until they run out of food!

MIRANDA: There are—

RACHEL: No good options. Yeah, yeah. I know.

(Pause. RED *stands up, putting the granola bar next to* CLARK.*)*

RED: I'll go.

CLARK: Not without eating your damn granola bar, you won't.

RED: Make me.

MIRANDA: I don't think that's a good idea.

RED: I know.

MIRANDA: If you get caught—

RED: Then you know they're close.

MIRANDA: They'll kill you. Or worse.

RED: I know.

MIRANDA: This is a stall, at best. You know that, right?

RACHEL: What does that mean?

MIRANDA: Say we find food. Enough to keep us going for a week. Let's get really crazy and say a month, even. What happens when it runs out again? It's not like anyone's bringing any more food in, and I sure as hell don't know how to farm.

RACHEL: It buys us time.

MIRANDA: For *what*?

RACHEL: To stay out of the hands of those alien fucks a little bit longer. To stay alive.

MIRANDA: Again. For what?

RACHEL: Because things might change.

MIRANDA: I highly doubt that.

RACHEL: But you don't know. Just like you didn't know aliens were going to show up in the first place. Besides, we're not just surviving. We're doing something, here. Letting people know what's going on, as best we can.

MIRANDA: Do you really think there's anyone listening?

RACHEL: There's at least a few. Clark's talking to them. Right?

CLARK: Right.

MIRANDA: A few.

RACHEL: That we know of.

MIRANDA: Right.

RACHEL: We can't just give up. Not yet.

(A long pause)

MIRANDA: Fine. Fine. But you shouldn't go alone, Red.

RED: Safer.

MIRANDA: Two people don't make much more noise than one. And that way we can carry more. Besides, if I stay in this room any longer, I think I might lose my mind.

RED: Fair.

RACHEL: Wait. Now you're going outside, too?

MIRANDA: If we're staying, we're staying. No sense half-assing it.

CLARK: Hold on a sec. *(He reaches under the desk the ham radio is sitting on, rummaging around until he comes up with a pair of walkie talkies.)* Here. Take one of these with you.

MIRANDA: Those might make noise. Give us away.

CLARK: Keep it turned off, then. Unless you need something. That way we can't blow your cover.

*(*CLARK *holds out a walkie to* RED. RED *takes it, and* CLARK *puts the granola bar in their hand, too.* RED *rolls their eyes, but sticks both in their pockets.)*

MIRANDA: If we don't come back…

RACHEL: Don't. Don't say that.

MIRANDA: If we don't, though—

RACHEL: You *will* come back--

MIRANDA: —*if* we don't, you have to get out of here as fast as you can. Even just to move elsewhere in town. If they take us alive, they might—

RACHEL: Miranda. You will come back. Okay?

MIRANDA: Rachel.

RACHEL: Be careful out there.

MIRANDA: Keep the door locked.

RACHEL: Will do.

*(*MIRANDA *gives* RACHEL *a look.)*

MIRANDA: *(To* CLARK*)* Keep the door locked.

CLARK: We will. Be careful.

RED: We will.

*(*RED *and* MIRANDA *exit. Reluctantly,* RACHEL *locks the door behind them.)*

RACHEL: They'll be okay.

*(*CLARK *looks at her a moment, then turns back to the radio.)*

Scene 5

(A couple of days later. We mostly hear static now, only a few isolated voices: "picking up survivors from the cities", "minimal remaining military activity".)

(Then: RACHEL *at the mic.* CLARK *sits at the ham station.)*

RACHEL: This is Rachel, 103.7 WCRP, with your usual morning update. First of all, and I'm sure you're tired of hearing this, if anyone has seen a pair of people foraging around the Cranberry Township area, and you have any way of getting word to us, we'd appreciate it. They've been gone a couple of days now. Or...if you've seen any of the aliens in the area, we'd appreciate hearing about that, too. I don't think our friends would've gone down without a fight, so most likely someone would've heard something. Anyway. According to the network, the aliens are starting to move outward from the city. They're picking through the ruins, looking for people—and bodies. Keep an eye out. Stay alive. *(She leans away, turning to* CLARK.*)*

RACHEL: Anything?

CLARK: Nothing. Hold on, I'll try again.

(CLARK pulls the headphone jack out of the rig, so the static is audible in the room.)

CLARK: This is Whiskey Three Lima Echo Sierra. Anyone read?

(Pause. Static)

CLARK: This is Whiskey Three Lima Echo Sierra. Yankee? Juliets? Bravo? Anybody?

NJ3JEN: Juliets here. I read you, Whiskey.

CLARK: Thank god. I was starting to wonder.

NJ3JEN: I was away from my mic—it's not the usual time.
I think Bravo's gone.

CLARK: What?

NJ3JEN: We… lived close to one another. Close-ish, anyway. There was a fire. I could see it from my window.

CLARK: What happened?

NJ3JEN: Dunno. Maybe Bravo set it, maybe the aliens tried to burn her out. Either way…

CLARK: Jesus. How did they find her?

NJ3JEN: They must've reached the area.

CLARK: We have people out there.

NJ3JEN: I know. I've been listening—is Rachel there?

RACHEL: Oh. Uh, I'm here.

NJ3JEN: Keep it up. It's nice to hear a voice, know I'm not alone.

RACHEL: Will do.

NJ3JEN: I'll let you know if I see any sign of them. And I'll check in tomorrow, regardless.
I hope they make it back safe.

CLARK: Thanks. 73, Juliets.

NJ3JEN: 73. Stay safe. Clear.

(Static. CLARK *turns it down so it's just barely audible. The drone of an alien ship.)*

CLARK: I can't believe…

RACHEL: Had you ever met her? Bravo?

CLARK: Eh. A couple of times, back before. She was a bit of a shut-in, though, mostly liked to keep things over the airwaves. Tough old bird.

RACHEL: I'm sorry.

CLARK: Yeah.
There's so few of us left.

RACHEL: Yeah.

(The alien ship passes overhead. Pause. RACHEL *gets up and starts to pace.)*

RACHEL: Try the walkie again.

CLARK: Rachel—

RACHEL: It can't hurt. Just.

CLARK: Okay. *(Into the walkie-talkie:)* Red? Miranda? You read us out there?

(Pause. Nothing)

CLARK: *(Into the walkie)* Even just click the talk button a few times if you can. Let us know you're out there.

(Nothing)

RACHEL: They should have been back by now.

CLARK: Well, let's think this through. Last we heard, they were out by the 7-11.

RACHEL: That's what, two, three miles?

CLARK: And it was already ransacked. You know how people are in a crisis.

RACHEL: How far do you think they'd go?

CLARK: Hard to say. These walkies only reach a few miles—they probably had to go out of range.

(Pause)

RACHEL: I should go look for them.

CLARK: Now, hold on—

RACHEL: They might be in trouble.

CLARK: And if they are? What would you do about it?

RACHEL: I don't know. But I can't just sit here.

CLARK: You wouldn't even know where to look. You'd just be compounding the problem, and for what?

RACHEL: So, what? We just wait?

CLARK: I don't see what else we can do.

(Pause)

RACHEL: I hate it when you're right.

CLARK: I know.

RACHEL: I hate hiding in here like a scared little turtle, huddled up inside the shell where it's safe. I feel like we should be doing something. Something more.

CLARK: We're getting information out there.

RACHEL: Yeah. If anyone's listening.

CLARK: More than most can do.

RACHEL: I guess.

(The radio crackles. Both jump. CLARK *turns to it, turning the volume back up.)*

KA2YO: —Yankee Oscar. Anybody read?

CLARK: Whiskey here. We read you, Yankee. A little early for you, isn't it?

KA2YO: You hearing this shit out of Baltimore?

CLARK: No. Too far for us. What are you hearing?

KA2YO: Sometimes I can pick up one of the stations down there. They've been quiet the past few days, but I just picked up a broadcast. It sounded like the DJ was urging people to turn themselves in.

CLARK: To the aliens?

KA2YO: Yeah. Call themselves "the Legion", apparently. They said if you turn yourself in, you won't be harmed. Only taken somewhere.

CLARK: Where?

KA2YO: They were vague on that front.

CLARK: You're not considering…

KA2YO: Me? Hah. That'll be the day. Just wanted to see if it sounded as crazy to anybody else as it does to me.

RACHEL: Those bastards.

KA2YO: Repeat, Whiskey?

CLARK: Nothing.

KA2YO: You all doing alright up there? Your friends turn up yet?

CLARK: No. Not yet.

KA2YO: Sorry to hear that.

RACHEL: They'll come back.

KA2YO: Say again?

CLARK: Nothing—

RACHEL: I said, they'll come back. They have to.

KA2YO: If you say so. Anyway, they're getting a little close for comfort, what with the whole Bravo situation, so I'll be out for the next little while. Just wanted you to know in case you don't hear from me for a bit.

CLARK: Thanks. 73.

KA2YO: Same to you.

(Static. CLARK *turns the radio back down.)*

RACHEL: Those fuckers. Those sneaky, underhanded fuckers. Do they really think we'll fall for that?

CLARK: Some folks probably will. If they're alone. If they're scared. Hungry. Tired. Might seem like the best option to some.

RACHEL: Cowards.

CLARK: No. Just people, trying to stay alive.

(A moment. RACHEL *deflates, sinking back into her chair.)*

RACHEL: "The Legion", huh?

CLARK: Wonder why.

RACHEL: Well, there's multiple kinds, right? The ones that fly, the ones that run. Probably more we haven't seen.

CLARK: Now there's a scary thought.

RACHEL: Why are they here? What do they want?

(A knock at the door. CLARK *and* RACHEL *freeze, staring at the door. A tense pause. Then, a knock again, this time in the "shave and a haircut" pattern.* RACHEL *jumps up and hurries to the door, opening it to reveal* RED*, a large bag slung over one shoulder. They are dirt-smeared and exhausted, but they are unharmed.)*

RACHEL: Holy shit.

*(*RED *grunts and moves past.* MIRANDA *appears in the door next, also laden with food.)*

RACHEL: I see you found food.

MIRANDA: Yeah. Among other things.

RACHEL: We were starting to think… Wait. What?

MIRANDA: *(Overlapping with* RACHEL*)* I know. *(To someone offstage)* Come on. Get inside, before another ship comes.

*(*MIRANDA *enters past* RACHEL*, and a moment later,* GWEN *follows her inside.)*

CLARK: Who in the hell are you?

MIRANDA: Rachel. Shut the door.

RACHEL: But—

MIRANDA: Shut the door.

*(*RACHEL *does.* GWEN *moves awkwardly into the space, trying not to trip over anything. She is carrying only a single backpack, full but not to bursting.)*

CLARK: Mind telling me who this person is you've just brought into my radio station?

MIRANDA: This is Gwen.

CLARK: Gwen.

MIRANDA: We, uh…ran into each other.

RACHEL: "Ran into each other"? Like you were just out for a casual stroll? What the hell, Miri? Where have you *been*?

MIRANDA: If I explain, will you not interrupt me?

RACHEL: Fine.

MIRANDA: Okay. The short version is that there was nothing left in the stores. We checked every single one Red could think of. Found a can here or there, but nothing substantial enough to be worth the trip. We spent…what, maybe a day?

*(*RED *nods.)*

MIRANDA: A day just going from store to store. Nothing.

RACHEL: So then where did all this come from?

MIRANDA: I'm getting to that. We ended up in a mostly residential area. We didn't see anyone. Not a single person moving out there other than us. They must be sweeping the area more than we thought, rounding people up somehow, because there's no one out there. And those ships going overhead every so often, just long enough in between them that you'd start to think maybe there wouldn't be another one.

RACHEL: Miri.

MIRANDA: And we were so hungry.

CLARK: What did you do?

MIRANDA: We broke into a house. We picked one that didn't have any cars in the driveway. No signs of life. Went around the back, found a window that hadn't been locked, and…

RACHEL: Holy shit.

MIRANDA: Found enough food for a couple of days at least, just in that first house.

CLARK: You stole it?

MIRANDA: It's not like they were using it. Desperate times and all that.

RACHEL: Did you like. Leave a note or something, at least?

MIRANDA: Why? For what? On the slim—and let me emphasize just how slim—chance that the owner of that house does eventually come back, somehow, do you really think they're going to be worried about a few missing cans?

RACHEL: Well, no, probably not—

MIRANDA: They'll assume someone needed them. Which we do, if we want to survive.

RACHEL: I just think that—

MIRANDA: Meanwhile, if the aliens found the note, they'd know there's someone left in the area. Maybe they'd look harder for us. Maybe they'd even have some way to track us back here. We have no idea what they're capable of, and I'd rather not find out when one comes knocking on our door.

RACHEL: Okay. Okay. I get it.

MIRANDA: Good.

CLARK: Did you actually see any aliens?

RED: Not really.

CLARK: Not really?

MIRANDA: We saw some in the sky, way off. But I don't think they ever saw us. Or else we probably wouldn't be here.

RACHEL: So how does, uh…

RED: Gwen.

RACHEL: Right. How does Gwen come in?

MIRANDA: She was hiding out in one of the houses we broke into. Almost out of food, too.

RACHEL: Whose idea was it to bring her back here? Yours, or Red's?

RED: She was alone.

MIRANDA: We both—we all decided.

CLARK: Don't remember getting a say, myself.

RACHEL: What happened to "we don't have enough food as it is"?

MIRANDA: You're the one who wanted to go out and help people.

RACHEL: And you're the one who didn't! So what changed?

MIRANDA: I guess I did.

RACHEL: You sure this isn't just about moving up the timeline?

MIRANDA: What do you mean?

RACHEL: Well, you want us to leave, right? And if we run out of supplies, we have to leave sooner.

MIRANDA: That's not—

RACHEL: So, you bring an extra person back. We run out of food faster. You get what you want.

MIRANDA: That's not why.

RACHEL: Convenient, though.

GWEN: *(Cutting in, matter-of-fact)* Do you want me to leave?

(Beat)

RACHEL: What?

GWEN: Do you want me to leave?

RACHEL: I didn't say that.

GWEN: You kind of did.

CLARK: We're all under a lot of pressure.

GWEN: No, yeah, I get that. I'm a strain on your resources. A stranger in your space. I get it. I really do. So: do you want me to leave?

RED: No.

MIRANDA: No.

GWEN: You two already made your choice. I wanna know what the others think.

(A pause)

RACHEL: No. I don't…no. I don't want you to leave. I won't lie and say I'm glad you're here—this room is getting pretty rank as it is, to be honest—but you are here. And you deserve shelter as much as anyone else.

GWEN: And you?

CLARK: Seems I'm outvoted, regardless.

GWEN: Maybe. But I'd like to know where we stand.

*(*CLARK *considers* GWEN *for a moment.)*

CLARK: Fuck it. If we're not in this together, what's the point of all this? Stay as long as you need to.

GWEN: Thank you. I really do appreciate it.

RACHEL: What were you doing out there alone? If you don't mind my asking. Seems like most people ran home to their families.

GWEN: I was in town on business when the aliens got here. Couldn't get home since all the airlines shut down. I took my rental car and got as far from the city as I could. Ran out of gas just as I hit 228, so I ditched the car and went to find somewhere to hole up.

RACHEL: Just like that, huh?

GWEN: What else was I supposed to do?

RACHEL: I dunno. Give up?

GWEN: I thought about it. Especially when the phones went out and I lost contact with my wife.

MIRANDA: Where is she?

GWEN: Chicago. So close, and yet so far, right? I was hoping things would die down and maybe I could refuel the rental car, get on the road, but…

CLARK: Have you been alone, all this time?

GWEN: …Yeah.

RACHEL: Jesus.

GWEN: What about all of you? What are you all doing in—what is this, a radio station?

RACHEL: The short version is that we're all a bunch of misfits who didn't have anywhere else to go.

MIRANDA: Speak for yourself. I was stranded here, same as you.

RACHEL: Yeah, yeah. And then we figured out that the aliens haven't taken out the radio, so we're just trying to keep information flowing while we can. Try to help anyone else who's still alive out there.

GWEN: You've been broadcasting this whole time?

RACHEL: Yep.

GWEN: And they haven't found you?
Don't get me wrong, I mean, it's a good thing they haven't. I just would've thought…

MIRANDA: Yeah. Me too. But maybe they just don't care enough to come after us.

RED: Seems unlikely.

CLARK: Or maybe we're too old-school for them.

MIRANDA: Riiiiight.

RACHEL: No, he has a point. Radio's pretty old-school even by human standards—maybe it's like hieroglyphics or something to aliens. They just can't understand it.

MIRANDA: Hieroglyphics?

CLARK: I think something like a Betamax tape would be a better metaphor. Most folks haven't had the equipment to play one of those in decades.

RACHEL: I've never even heard of a Betamax tape.

CLARK: Exactly.

MIRANDA: Maybe.

RACHEL: Whatever the reason, doesn't seem like they're coming.

GWEN: Do you think anyone's listening? Any humans, I mean.

RACHEL: There's at least a couple of Clark's nerdy ham friends still out there.

CLARK: *(With no actual heat)* Hey.

GWEN: That's it?

RACHEL: That we know of. There might be more.

GWEN: Do you really think so?

(Brief pause)

RED: We hope so.

(Another, more awkward pause. GWEN *shifts her bag on her shoulders.)*

GWEN: Where should I…?

RACHEL: Oh, uh, wherever, I guess.

*(*GWEN *picks a spot tentatively.)*

GWEN: This isn't gonna be over anytime soon, is it?

RACHEL: No. Probably not.

GWEN: At least it's nice not to be alone.

MIRANDA: Yeah. It is.

Scene 6

(Several weeks later. The radio is entirely static now, with only faint suggestions of what might be voices, and might be our imaginations.)

(Lights up on RACHEL *at the mic.)*

(The room should look thoroughly lived-in by now. Each person has staked out their own little space, with one main pile of blankets serving as the main bed, with a couple of other smaller cushions scattered around. A new garbage bag

has appeared, and a stack of cans against one wall shows how much food they've gone through. A couple of bulbs have burned out, or been taken out. A couple of pieces of nonessential equipment are dark.)

*(*CLARK *is at his ham station.* GWEN *is lying in the pile of blankets, absently watching* RACHEL. RED *sits against the wall near* CLARK*, staring into the middle distance.* MIRANDA *paces. Everyone is dressed warmly, like the heat isn't quite working right.)*

RACHEL: For anyone who might be just tuning in, this is Rachel with what once was 103.7 WCRP. Still is, for what it's worth. This is your morning update. We are…what, three, four weeks into this whole alien occupation thing? I've lost track. No major updates for today, other than that the Legion—that's the aliens, if anyone's missed that particular memo—continues to search the area. Not sure if they know there's still people out here, or if they're just the thorough types. I also don't know if they can hear us and just can't find us, or don't care, or what. Anyway. Stay safe out there. Stay alive.

*(*RACHEL *sits back, rubbing at her face. A moment. Static from the ham setup.)*

MIRANDA: I don't know why you still bother with that.

RACHEL: We've been over this.

MIRANDA: 'Someone has to get the word out.' Right. Even though we haven't seen anyone else in weeks.

RACHEL: Just because we haven't seen them doesn't mean there's no one there.

GWEN: *(A genuine question)* Do you actually believe that?

RACHEL: If we can make it this long, others could, too.

MIRANDA: You're not even giving any useful information. We haven't heard from anyone in days.

RACHEL: It doesn't matter. They need to know we're still here.

MIRANDA: Whatever.

(Pause)

GWEN: It's too quiet in here.

MIRANDA: What is there left to talk about?

GWEN: Hmm.
How about this. If you were an animal, what animal would you be?

RACHEL: What?

MIRANDA: What kind of corporate icebreaker question is that?

GWEN: I think I'd be some kind of bird, personally.

CLARK: And why is that?

GWEN: I dunno, just a feeling. Probably not a bird of prey, though. What about you?

CLARK: Hmm. Never gave it much thought before.

MIRANDA: I can't believe we're having this conversation right now.

CLARK: What do you think, Red? *(Pause)* Red?

RED: *(As if coming out of a daze)* Hm?

CLARK: If I were an animal, what would I be? Or hell, answer for yourself.

RED: Hm.

RACHEL: Oh my god.

RED: What animal would I be, or what animal would I want to be?

CLARK: Your question, Gwen.

GWEN: Hmmm. Whichever.

RED: I'd want to be a mongoose.

RACHEL: Why?

MIRANDA: Not you, too.

RED: They're little, but tough. They can take on cobras and shit.

GWEN: No kidding?

*(*RED *nods.)*

RACHEL: I think you'd be a badger, Clark.

CLARK: Yeah?

RACHEL: Yeah. I'm feeling badger.

CLARK: How dare you. I'm clearly a bear. An old, hairy, grumpy gay man? It was right there.

RACHEL: Fine. What kind of bear, though?

RED: Sun bear.

CLARK: Aren't those the goofy looking ones?

*(*RED *just grins.)*

MIRANDA: I think badger suits you better, Rachel.

RACHEL: Really?

MIRANDA: You get your teeth into something and just won't let go. Even when you probably should.

RACHEL: What does that make you?

MIRANDA: I don't know. What does that make me?

(A pause as they all consider MIRANDA.*)*

MIRANDA: I regret this already.

RACHEL: A swan.

MIRANDA: That's…nicer than I expected.

RACHEL: I'm not wrong.

MIRANDA: Thanks? I think.

GWEN: I'll claim duck, then. Just floating along, eating bread crumbs. Sounds nice right about now.

(A pause. The radio crackles.)

KA2YO: Kilo Alpha Two Yankee Oscar here. Whiskey, you read me?

CLARK: We read you. Have you heard from Juliets lately?

KA2YO: No. Was hoping you had. They must've gotten her.

CLARK: Damn.

KA2YO: Guess it's just you and me left, old man.

CLARK: Do you need anything? Supplies? Maybe we could get something to you.

KA2YO: I'm alright. I prepared for this, unlike the rest of you.

CLARK: For aliens?

KA2YO: Well no, not specifically. But for shit to get bad. If I could just get the damn repeater working, I'd be right as rain.

CLARK: No luck, huh?

KA2YO: Needs a new duplexer, and wouldn't you know, I can't exactly go out and buy one.

CLARK: I'll have a look around, see if I can scare one up.

KA2YO: Nah. Wouldn't be safe to bring it to me, anyway.

CLARK: If you're sure. Anything new we should tell folks?

KA2YO: No. I'll let you know if that changes.

CLARK: Got it. Thanks, Yankee.

KA2YO: 73, Whiskey.

(Static. The mood in the room has darkened. RED *gets up, grabs a heavier coat.)*

RACHEL: Where are you going?

RED: To take a look around. Clear the leaves off the solar panels.

MIRANDA: Didn't we just—

CLARK: Be careful.

*(*RED *nods. Exits.* MIRANDA *locks the door behind them.)*

CLARK: I'm worried about that kid.

MIRANDA: Then why encourage them?

CLARK: Doesn't matter if I do or not. They're grown, they can make their own decisions.

MIRANDA: It's a stupid risk, going outside so much.

CLARK: Least it means someone's keeping an eye out. And they've got the best chance of any of us of staying unseen.

MIRANDA: Always looking on the bright side.

CLARK: Only in comparison to you, my dear.

*(*MIRANDA *makes a face at him, goes over to inventory the food.)*

GWEN: *(Re: the ham setup)* Down to one, now. Right?

CLARK: Seems that way. Damn.

RACHEL: How well did you know Juliets?

CLARK: Not very. She was new. Only picked up the hobby…maybe a year ago? Still. I always liked talking with her.

RACHEL: Not to mention she had the best vantage point into the downtown area.

CLARK: Right.

GWEN: Wonder who'll go next. Your friend Yankee, or us.

RACHEL: Don't say that.

MIRANDA: No, she's right. It's only a matter of time, at this point.

RACHEL: You've said that from the beginning.

MIRANDA: That doesn't make it any less true. *(She stops digging through the bags.)* We're down to our last couple of days of food. Again.

RACHEL: So we'll get more.

MIRANDA: Easy for you to say when you're not the one looking. We have to go further and further each time we go out to get more, and we get less and less that we can actually use. Not to mention the weather's getting colder.

RACHEL: We'll—

MIRANDA: Uh.

RACHEL: Fine. *You'll* find more. You always have in the past.

MIRANDA: That's what I'm saying. We've gotten lucky, up until now. But our luck is bound to run out, whether it's not being able to find any more food, or finally being spotted and captured.

CLARK: Or worse.

MIRANDA: I think we need to seriously consider making a run for it.

RACHEL: You don't even know if that military base is still standing. Those are one of the first things the Legion targeted.

MIRANDA: They're also fortified to withstand that kind of attack.

RACHEL: In theory, sure. Against human weapons.

MIRANDA: They're certainly sturdier than a radio station basement.

RACHEL: More of a target, too.

GWEN: What's this about a military base?

MIRANDA: East of here. A couple hundred miles.

GWEN: Ah.
There's also the option of going to the Legion.

MIRANDA/RACHEL: *(Simultaneously) What?*

RACHEL: You know about that?

CLARK: I may have mentioned it.

GWEN: I'm just saying. They say if you go to them, you won't be harmed.

RACHEL: And you believe them?

GWEN: ...I don't know. Would they lie?

RACHEL: Sure. To save themselves the trouble of hunting us down.

GWEN: I guess. It's an option. That's all.

MIRANDA: No, it's not.

CLARK: If the rest of you leave...it's one I'll have to consider.

RACHEL: We won't put you in that position.

CLARK: We'll see.

RACHEL: Clark...

CLARK: It's alright, Rachel. Sometimes all you have left are bad options and worse ones.

RACHEL: *(To* MIRANDA*)* When did you get so gung-ho about the military, anyway? Didn't think you were a fan.

MIRANDA: I'm not, but...

RACHEL: But?

MIRANDA: The last time I heard from Jess, they were heading to a fort south of San Jose.

RACHEL: *That's* what this is about?

(Before MIRANDA *can answer, an urgent knock at the door, in the usual rhythm.* MIRANDA *opens it for* RED.*)*

RED: One of them is coming.

MIRANDA: What?

RACHEL: How?

GWEN: When?

RED: An alien. Don't know how, but it's heading right for us. Almost looks like it's following a trail.

RACHEL: What, like footprints or something?

RED: No idea. No time.

GWEN: Do we run?

RACHEL: Why don't we just lock the door, keep quiet?

MIRANDA: And if it breaks down the door? Then what? We'll be cornered in here.

RACHEL: There's five of us, and only one of it. Right, Red?

RED: That I saw.

MIRANDA: We're unarmed. And I certainly don't know how to fight. Do any of you?

GWEN: Does a blue belt in karate from twenty years ago count?

MIRANDA: We run.

CLARK: I can't.

RACHEL: Okay. New plan. Clark holes up here, the rest of us scatter. It can't follow all of us.

MIRANDA: And the one it does follow?

RACHEL: It's that or try to fight it. Maybe if we can get the drop on it, we can take it.

GWEN: I like that better than just sitting here, letting it come to us.

RACHEL: Is that the plan, then?

(A moment. They all look at each other.)

RACHEL: Run, or fight?

RED: Fight.

GWEN: Fight. I think with four of us on one, we have a chance.

MIRANDA: That's assuming there is only one.

RACHEL: If not, we're fucked regardless. If we ran, they'd just split up and chase us down.

MIRANDA: Good point.
Fight.

RACHEL: Let's see what we can find upstairs before it gets here.

*(*RED, GWEN, *and* RACHEL *exit.* MIRANDA *pauses in the door.)*

MIRANDA: Keep this door closed until we knock. No matter what you hear.

CLARK: Right.
Good luck.

MIRANDA: Thanks.

*(*MIRANDA *closes the door behind her.* CLARK *locks it.)*

Scene 7

*(*CLARK*, alone in the room. Listening. The room is utterly still and silent, except for the faint static of the ham radio rig. He holds out his hands in front of him, watching them shake. He clenches his fists. A long moment. He turns to the radio.)*

CLARK: Yankee, do you read? *(Pause)* Yankee, this is Whiskey Three Lima Echo Sierra. If you can hear me, answer, you bastard.

(Pause. Nothing)

(Then, something crashes against the door. CLARK *freezes. Muffled thumping from the other side of the door. Then, the usual knock.)*

*(*CLARK *wipes his hands on his pants. Stands. Makes his way to the door and opens it.)*

*(*MIRANDA, GWEN, *and* RACHEL *enter, all carrying* RED. *They all are scraped and bruised, but* RED *is by far the worst off, their torso and hands covered in blood.)*

MIRANDA: First aid kit. Quickly.

CLARK: R-right, right.

(While the others settle RED *on the floor,* CLARK *finds a first aid kit and brings it to* MIRANDA.*)*

MIRANDA: Where does it hurt?

RED: E-everywhere. But…

*(*RED*'s hands go to their stomach.* MIRANDA *carefully peels their shirt away, revealing a large, deep gash.)*

MIRANDA: Oh shit.

CLARK: What happened?

RACHEL: We won, believe it or not.

CLARK: This is what winning looks like?

RACHEL: We're still alive. More than I can say for the other guy.

MIRANDA: I need someone on the kit.

GWEN: I got it.

*(*GWEN *goes to her knees next to* MIRANDA*, opening up the kit.)*

MIRANDA: *(To* GWEN*)* Gauze, cleanser, anything we could use to close the wound up. *(To* RACHEL *and* CLARK*)* Towels. Blankets. Something to stop the bleeding.

*(*RACHEL *grabs a blanket from the corner, brings it over.* MIRANDA *takes it.)*

MIRANDA: *(To* RED*)* This is going to hurt.

*(*RED *nods, gritting their teeth.* MIRANDA *scrubs the blanket across their stomach, trying to clean away the blood.)*

MIRANDA: Fuck. Fuck. That's deep.
Okay. Stop the bleeding. I need a fresh blanket. As clean as possible.

*(*RACHEL *grabs another.* MIRANDA *balls it up and presses it into* RED*'s stomach, hard, trying to hold the gash together as she does.)*

RED: *(Breathlessly)* Fuuuuck.

MIRANDA: I know. I'm sorry.

RED: I'm gonna—I need to—

MIRANDA: Stay as still as you can.

*(*CLARK *grabs the nearest soft thing—could be a jacket, pillow, blanket, it doesn't matter—and moves to kneel by* RED*'s head, cushioning them as best he can.)*

CLARK: What happened?

GWEN: We jumped it. It didn't look that tough—little bugger maybe a foot shorter than Red. Nasty looking thing. Didn't look armed, but its claws were enough to do…that.

CLARK: How did you…

RACHEL: Kill it? Bashed its head in while Red held it down. I have no idea how they did it—the fucker was squirming like a pissed off cat.

GWEN: Let me know when you need this stuff, Miranda.

MIRANDA: We have to stop the bleeding first. That's the most important thing.

RACHEL: Putting that first aid training to good use, huh?

MIRANDA: What little I remember of it.

*(*MIRANDA *shifts their grip on the blanket.* RED *hisses in pain. They've started to breathe hard, head falling back against the cushion.)*

MIRANDA: They're going into shock.

RED: I'm gonna puke…

MIRANDA: Please don't.

RED: I'm gonna…

MIRANDA: Clark, if they puke, turn their head to the side. Make sure they don't choke.

CLARK: Okay.

MIRANDA: Rachel, can you elevate their legs?

RACHEL: Sure, sure.

(She does, tucking whatever she can find beneath their legs. MIRANDA *checks under the blanket—the bleeding hasn't slowed. She bears down harder with the pressure.* RED *barely reacts.)*

MIRANDA: Shit. Shit, shit.

GWEN: What can we do?

MIRANDA: Check their pulse.

(GWEN puts two fingers to the side of RED's neck. A moment.)

GWEN: It's fast, but it feels weak.

RACHEL: That's not good.

MIRANDA: I don't…even if we had an ambulance on the way, I don't know what else they could do. They're losing a lot of blood, and even if we could stop the bleeding, they're in shock. Plus I think those claws cut more than just skin.

(RED raises a shaky hand towards CLARK. CLARK catches it, holding it between his own.)

CLARK: Hang on, kid.

RED: S-sorry…

CLARK: Nothing to be sorry for.

GWEN: Miranda, you're bleeding, too. *(She points to a cut down the side of MIRANDA's arm.)*

MIRANDA: It's fine. It can wait.

(RED's head lolls to the side—they've lost consciousness.)

MIRANDA: Check them again, Gwen?

(She does. A long moment)

GWEN: I'm not—I'm not sure. My heart is pounding.

MIRANDA: Switch with me.

(They do, GWEN holding down the blanket while MIRANDA checks for a pulse. Another long moment.)

CLARK: Red?

(MIRANDA sits back on her heels. She shakes her head slowly.)

MIRANDA: I don't feel anything.

CLARK: No.

MIRANDA: I'm sorry.

RACHEL: God.

MIRANDA: You can let go of the blanket, Gwen.

GWEN: Are you…are you sure?

MIRANDA: At most, it's delaying the inevitable.

RACHEL: Miranda—

MIRANDA: It's over.

(Reluctantly, GWEN *lets go of the blanket. It's soaked. She shakily takes* RED*'s other hand.)*

CLARK: What are you doing?

GWEN: I don't want them to be alone. When they go.

RACHEL: They're not.

GWEN: I know. But if they're still in there, I want them to be able to feel it. Feel us.

(A moment. RACHEL *rests her hand on* RED*'s leg.* MIRANDA *slumps down beside them. For a moment, they should all be physically in contact with* RED*. It is silent, except for the ever-present static of the radio.)*

CLARK: This isn't how it was supposed to go.

GWEN: I don't think this is how any of us expected things to go.

CLARK: No, I mean. They were supposed to run this place, when they were ready. If we hadn't gone under. I was going to give it to them.

RACHEL: Clark…

CLARK: I was supposed to go first.

(A long, quiet moment. Then, GWEN *gently sets* RED*'s hand down.)*

GWEN: Miranda. Let me take a look at your arm.

MIRANDA: …Yeah. Okay.

(Over the next couple of pages, GWEN *tends to* MIRANDA*'s arm—cleaning it, bandaging it, etc.* RACHEL *gets a clean blanket and lays it gently over* RED*, then sits next to* CLARK.*)*

CLARK: This is all wrong.

RACHEL: I know. I'm sorry.

GWEN: This'll sting.

MIRANDA: Ow.

GWEN: Sorry, sorry.

RACHEL: Maybe we should've run.

CLARK: Doesn't matter now.

RACHEL: No, I guess it doesn't.

CLARK: They're dead. And for what?

RACHEL: Nothing. Sometimes that's how it goes in a war, I guess.

CLARK: Is that what this is? A war?

RACHEL: Can't think what else we would call it at this point.

CLARK: We're not soldiers.

RACHEL: I'm not sure that matters now. If it ever did.

(Pause)

MIRANDA: The alien. When it first showed up. It was acting weird.

RACHEL: How do we know what weird is for an alien?

MIRANDA: No, it was something…I can't quite put my finger on it.

GWEN: Smelling. It was scenting the air.

(They all look at GWEN.*)*

GWEN: My dad used to have a hunting dog. When it was tracking…it looked like that.

MIRANDA: They track by scent. That's good to know.

RACHEL: Not sure it was worth dying over.

MIRANDA: No.

(Pause)

RACHEL: Should we maybe, like…take its stuff? Looked like it had some fancy gadgets.

MIRANDA: That might have tracking devices in them. Plus, we have no idea how to use them.

RACHEL: You're right. You're right. *(Pause)* What do we do now?

MIRANDA: We get ready to leave.

RACHEL: You're really going to do this now.

MIRANDA: If one of them found us, others can, too.

RACHEL: And? Nothing else has changed since the last time we had this argument.

MIRANDA: Except that one of us is dead. And we've left a trail of blood leading right to our hiding spot.

RACHEL: There are cleaning supplies upstairs.

MIRANDA: Okay, so they follow the smell of bleach instead. Besides, do you really want to stay in the same room where someone just died?

CLARK: We have to bury them.
Leave if you have to. But first, we have to bury them.

(Pause)

MIRANDA: We don't…we don't have a shovel.

CLARK: There's one in the workroom. I don't even remember why.

MIRANDA: That's a lot of time outside. Exposed.

CLARK: In the woods out back, then. Tonight, when it's dark.

RACHEL: Come on, Miranda. It's the least we can do for them now.

MIRANDA: Alright. Alright.

GWEN: I'll clean up here. Red and…the rest.

MIRANDA: We'll be back once the hole is dug.

CLARK: I'm coming with you. Someone has to show you where the shovel is. And where the…where the earth is soft.

*(*MIRANDA *nods. She,* CLARK, *and* RACHEL *exit.)*

Scene 8

(The next day. RACHEL, *at the mic. The space has been cleaned up as best it can—the first aid kit packed away, the bloody blankets and* RED*'s body removed. There may still be a stain on the floor.* CLARK *is in what remains of the pile of blankets, trying to sleep.* MIRANDA *is at the ham station, headset on one ear and off the other.* GWEN *sits against the wall, looking exhausted.)*

RACHEL: This is Rachel. 103.7 WCRP. Sorry if we scared you, going silent like that. We had a bit of a…an alien showed up at our door. One of the ground units. We still don't know much about it, but I can tell you that it was smaller than a human. It was searching alone, or appeared to be. I can tell you that it appeared to be tracking by scent, so if you're hiding out there, be careful to cover your tracks very, very thoroughly. I can tell you that it didn't have anything we could identify as a weapon, but it did have extremely sharp claws.

I want you all to have this information, because a friend of mine died for it. Red wasn't a fighter. Hell, they weren't much of a talker, half the time. If you'd asked me before all this happened, I would've sworn up and down that they hated me. Maybe they did. But going through something like this together? It changes you. They were smart—so fucking smart—and they cared more than they liked to let on. And they're dead, because these aliens just won't leave us the hell alone. But because of them, the rest of us are still alive to remember them. And I want to make sure the rest of you remember them, too. Remember that they were here, and they mattered, even if they'd have rather spent the day with their gadgets than other people. Remember that, even if you've never fought a day in your life, it's never too late to throw the first punch. Remember Red, who went down fighting to the last. *(She leans away from the mic, hits the mute.)*

MIRANDA: You make them sound like a hero.

RACHEL: Is there a problem with that?

MIRANDA: It's…it doesn't feel right.

RACHEL: Why?

MIRANDA: Because. They weren't a hero. They were just a person, and they died.

RACHEL: They kept the rest of us alive, didn't they? Seems pretty heroic to me.

MIRANDA: It's just…it was so hectic. So chaotic. It could have been any one of us.

RACHEL: But it wasn't. It was Red.
Besides. People listening need a reminder that one person can make a difference. That it is worth fighting back.

MIRANDA: Red died hurting, Rachel. They died scared, and confused, and in pain.

RACHEL: I know that. I was here, too.

CLARK: *(Sitting up)* We all were.

MIRANDA: This isn't some fantasy where the hero goes down in a blaze of glory. You can't make this any better by spinning it.

RACHEL: I'm a DJ. That's what I do.

MIRANDA: Red deserves better than to be reduced to a story for your...whatever you're doing.

RACHEL: I'm not "reducing" anything—or anyone. Don't tell me how to fucking grieve when you barely even knew them.

MIRANDA: As if you were such good friends? How long did you know them? Do you even know their last name?

GWEN: *(Interrupting)* Look. The message is out. It's done. Alright? So just...drop it.

RACHEL: Fine by me.

MIRANDA: Fine.

(A moment)

CLARK: S'weird.

GWEN: What is?

CLARK: They never said much, but...it's too damn quiet in here without them.

RACHEL: I know what you mean.

GWEN: I feel like I still barely knew them.

CLARK: Sometimes I still feel—felt. Felt that way, too.

RACHEL: I think you knew them better than anyone in the world.

CLARK: I guess I did.

GWEN: Tell me about them?

CLARK: I wouldn't know where to start.

MIRANDA: How'd they start working here? Kind of a weird gig for someone their age.

RACHEL: Miranda.

CLARK: No, she's right. Radio these days is mostly old fogies like me and Phil and true believers like this one. *(He indicates* RACHEL.*)*

MIRANDA: So?

CLARK: I'd seen them around town a few times. Cranberry Township isn't that big. And then one day, we'd been having a lot of technical difficulties, and they just… knocked on the door. Said they needed a job, liked fixing old things. I said I'd take them on on a trial basis, and the rest is history.

GWEN: That's it?

CLARK: Pretty much. We just…clicked. Weren't even a year in before I finally knew who I was going to give this place to.

(A pause)

CLARK: *(To* MIRANDA*)* Have you heard anything?

MIRANDA: No. It's been silent.

CLARK: Have you tried other frequencies?

MIRANDA: Still nothing.

CLARK: Yankee must really be gone, then. There's no one left in the network.

RACHEL: Doesn't mean there's no one listening.

CLARK: No. But.
I never expected to be the only one left.

RACHEL: Yeah.

(Pause)

GWEN: I think I should go.

RACHEL: What?

MIRANDA: Go? Go where?

GWEN: I'm not totally sure, but I'm leaning towards the Legion.

RACHEL: You've got to be fucking kidding me.

GWEN: No.

MIRANDA: Why would you do that? And why now?

GWEN: Because I froze. During the fight.
The rest of you were going at that alien with everything you had, and I had the crowbar in my hand, and I had a clear shot, and I just… didn't swing. I couldn't move.
Maybe if I'd swung, Red would still be alive.

RACHEL: You can't blame yourself for that.

GWEN: Can't I?

MIRANDA: It's in the past.

GWEN: But we'll have to fight again. Almost certainly. And I'm more of a liability than anything else. I don't know how all your radio gadgets work. Miranda's got the first aid covered. I don't have anything in particular to offer.

RACHEL: You don't have to have anything to offer. You don't have to be "useful." You deserve as much safety and shelter as any of us do.

GWEN: That's a nice sentiment. But you said it yourself: this is a war. And in war, you have to ration your resources. Make sure you can make it through to the end.
There's Legion east of here, right? I'll head that way, see if I can find out for sure if they're fibbing about taking people alive.

MIRANDA: Gwen. You can't seriously be doing this.

GWEN: You don't need me here. You didn't want me here in the first place.

RACHEL: That's not—

GWEN: I'm not blaming you. Or judging you. I was—still am, really—a stranger to all of you.

CLARK: What if going to them helps them find this place?

RACHEL: That's true. They could track you. Or make you talk.

GWEN: I…hadn't thought about that. I could say that I'd die first, but I really don't know that for sure, do I? *(A pause)* I don't know. I can't stay here anymore. I just…can't.

RACHEL: I mean…we can't make you. Or won't, rather.

CLARK: This is supposed to be a safe house, not a prison.

GWEN: I'll do whatever I can not to endanger you. Cover my tracks, at the very least.

MIRANDA: Why not go to the base instead? I have maps, screenshots—I can give them to you.

GWEN: Well…my wife wouldn't have fought, as much as she would've wanted to. She'd have gone quietly, for the sake of our kid.

MIRANDA: Oh.
You never told us their names.

GWEN: Marcie. That's my wife. And Aiden.

MIRANDA: If you have the chance, keep an eye out for a Jess from San Jose, will you?

GWEN: Yeah.

RACHEL: You can't.

GWEN: I can, and I am.

CLARK: At least take a little food with you. For the road.

GWEN: Okay. But only a little.

*(*GWEN *accepts some food and a bottle of water, putting them into the backpack she arrived with. She moves to the door.)*

GWEN: Good luck.

RACHEL: You, too.

Scene 9

*(*RACHEL *at the mic. She unmutes the mic. Pauses. Takes a deep breath.)*

RACHEL: This is 103.7, WCRP. We're…what, a month and a half, two months? Into the Legion occupation. Don't have much news for you tonight. We haven't heard an alien ship in a couple of days, which suggests that maybe they've moved on from the area. Or maybe they're just getting sneakier. Hard to say. It's been several weeks since we've seen or heard from anybody else in the area, but we're hanging in there. I hope you all are, too.

(She hesitates, then mutes the mic. MIRANDA *looks up from where she's scanning through the ham frequencies.* CLARK *is off to the side, eating a granola bar while he flips idly through a book. Everyone is bundled up even more—*CLARK *is wrapped in a blanket. The lights are even dimmer than before.)*

RACHEL: Anything?

*(*MIRANDA *shakes their head.)*

RACHEL: Yeah, I didn't think so.

MIRANDA: I think it's safe to say that there isn't anyone still in range.

RACHEL: At least, no one who has the equipment to respond.

MIRANDA: Sure.

CLARK: What if we could extend our range?

RACHEL: What?

MIRANDA: How? This station can only reach what, thirty to forty miles on a good day?

CLARK: Right, but we've got a ham setup right here, and that can go a lot further.

MIRANDA: We're not getting any response on the ham, either.

CLARK: True. But what if I told you I know where we can find a repeater? And we wouldn't even have to move it.

RACHEL: I'm listening.

CLARK: Yankee had one. And I just so happen to have the part it needs. Found it in the storage room when I went for more toilet paper the other day.

MIRANDA: Sounds a little too good to be true.

CLARK: Well, there is a catch.

MIRANDA: Uh-huh.

CLARK: Yankee's been, uh…been gone a while. We'll need to clean off their solar rig. And they're a good few miles from here.

RACHEL: Is the repair something you'd have to do yourself, Clark?

CLARK: Yes.

MIRANDA: Okay, so we're talking several hours' walk, at least. Not to mention we have no idea if there are more Legion in the area.

CLARK: Isn't it worth trying, at least?

MIRANDA: For what?
Do you really, honestly think we're going to reach anyone?

RACHEL: I do.

MIRANDA: I wasn't asking you.

(Pause)

CLARK: I think we have to try.

MIRANDA: Why?

RACHEL: Because if we don't, isn't that just giving up?

MIRANDA: So what if it is? All the ham folks are gone. Red is gone. Gwen is gone. Isn't that enough loss?

RACHEL: You barely even knew them. Any of them.

MIRANDA: Still.

(Pause. RACHEL *folds her arms.* MIRANDA *sighs.)*

MIRANDA: It doesn't matter what I say, does it?

RACHEL: I think you're outvoted.

MIRANDA: Fine. Whatever. You're both adults—you want to throw your lives away, I can't stop you. *(She turns back to the ham setup, flicking through a couple more frequencies almost absently. Then, she stiffens.)* Woah.

RACHEL/CLARK: What?

MIRANDA: I'm getting something—hold on.

(She pulls out the headphone jack. The signal is staticky at first, distorted, but clears enough to be understood when MIRANDA *tweaks the frequency.)*

EMERGENCY BROADCAST: —Fort Lee. Repeat, emergency civilian shelter available at Fort Lee. Please bring government-issued ID and no more than one small piece of luggage. Emergency civilian shelter available at Fort Lee. Repeat, emergency civilian shelter available at Fort Lee. Please bring government-issued ID…

(MIRANDA *turns the volume down.)*

MIRANDA: Holy shit.

RACHEL: That's just an automated system. It doesn't mean anything.

MIRANDA: Then why are we only just hearing it now?

RACHEL: Are you sure you've checked that frequency before?

MIRANDA: …Yes.

RACHEL: Are you *sure*?

MIRANDA: I must have. Or Clark.

CLARK: I checked all of them. I think.

RACHEL: Or maybe the weather changed, and now it's reaching us for the first time. The weather can affect the range, right?

CLARK: Sure.

RACHEL: Where the hell even is Fort Lee?

MIRANDA: Just south of Richmond.

RACHEL: That's even further than the one you were talking about.

MIRANDA: Yes, but—

RACHEL: Did you get screenshots for that?

MIRANDA: No. But I bet Clark has maps, right?

CLARK: I do.

RACHEL: You have no way of knowing if there's even anyone left. That could just be an old announcement they didn't bother to disable.

MIRANDA: Don't you think the Legion would've destroyed it, if they'd attacked?

RACHEL: Or—maybe they left it as a lure. Every person who walks in on their own is one more they don't have to hunt down, right?

MIRANDA: I...hadn't thought of that. But wouldn't that mean they'd figured out the radio?

RACHEL: Even if we could make it that far—which, let me be clear, *we* can't—we could just be walking into a trap.

MIRANDA: At least we'd be doing something other than...

RACHEL: What?

MIRANDA: Talking to the air. To people who aren't even there anymore. At least this way it'd be over, one way or the other.

RACHEL: Fuck that. I'm not walking into the Legion's hands after all this. No fucking way. And Clark—

MIRANDA: I know. I know.

RACHEL: There have to be more people out there. They're just out of range. We need to turn the repeater on.

MIRANDA: It's too dangerous.

RACHEL: What happened to "I can't stop you"?

MIRANDA: Now we have a lead. An actual, tangible lead—somewhere we can go where we *know* there are people.

CLARK: Were.

MIRANDA: Fine. We know there were people, at some point. Which is more than we know about the hypothetical people we might be reaching if we turn on the damn repeater.

RACHEL: You aren't even considering it. You've wanted to run from the start, regardless of how much good we're doing.

MIRANDA: How much we *might* be doing.

RACHEL: And if we run to the military, we're definitely not doing anyone any good.

MIRANDA: We'd be keeping ourselves safe.

RACHEL: And that's more important to you?

MIRANDA: Than whatever small amount of good we might be doing for the hypothetical people you imagine are still listening? Yes!

RACHEL: You're so fucking—never mind. Never mind.

MIRANDA: No, what?

RACHEL: Selfish.

MIRANDA: *I'm* selfish? You're the one who's putting us all in danger to sit here and pretend you're being some kind of hero. Do you actually think you're doing anything here, Rachel? Or are you just stroking your own ego even though it might cost us all our lives?

RACHEL: This has nothing to do with my ego.

MIRANDA: Maybe not. Maybe you're just too attached to the idea that there might be someone out there, and you can't fucking let it go. Or maybe you're scared.

RACHEL: Of what?

MIRANDA: You tell me.

RACHEL: We don't all cut and run when something isn't working out, Miranda.

MIRANDA: Fine. Let's say I am being selfish. Why not be fucking selfish at a time like this? We tried to help. We really, truly did. But what good will staying here to die do at this point?

RACHEL: We're doing fine!

MIRANDA: Not all of us!

CLARK: Alright, enough! *(Pause)* You both need to take some time to calm down.

RACHEL: But—

CLARK: All you're doing right now is hurting each other. We don't have to decide anything tonight. Nothing is going to change in the next 12 hours.

MIRANDA: Fine.

RACHEL: Fine.

CLARK: Good. Both of you, get some sleep. I'll keep an ear on the radio.

(They settle on opposite sides of the stage. CLARK *settles in at the ham station. The low buzz of static)*

(Time passes. RACHEL *and* MIRANDA *are asleep.* CLARK *stands slowly, carefully. He picks up a toolkit from among the bags and other debris in the room. Then, as quietly as he can, he exits.)*

(Depending on the staging, we may see a moment where RACHEL *and* MIRANDA *wake up some time later, realize* CLARK *is gone, and go after him. Feel free to ad-lib a couple of expletives if need be.)*

Scene 10

(The room is empty. For a long moment, there is no sound other than the faint rise and fall of radio static from the ham station.)

(Then, MIRANDA *and* RACHEL *enter. Both look exhausted.* MIRANDA *retrieves a bottle of water, while* RACHEL *goes to the ham station, collapsing into the chair. She puts her head in her hands.)*

RACHEL: I should've known. I should've fucking known. He's always been such a stubborn bastard.

MIRANDA: If he was determined to go—

RACHEL: We couldn't have stopped him. Or wouldn't, anyway. But we could've at least gone with him. Been with him.

MIRANDA: And disappeared right along with him.

RACHEL: At least then we'd know what the hell happened. As it is...

MIRANDA: Yeah.

RACHEL: I'm so fucking tired of not knowing.

MIRANDA: What about the walkie?

*(*RACHEL *checks the storage area.)*

RACHEL: He didn't even take one.

MIRANDA: He knew.

RACHEL: Yeah. I think he did. *(She takes a deep breath. Then starts tuning through the frequencies.)*

MIRANDA: What are you doing?

RACHEL: Seeing if he did it.

MIRANDA: If he did do it, will that make it worth it?

RACHEL: No.

(A new voice comes over the radio.)

WARNING: —stay away from Meridian. Repeat, stay away from Meridian. The aliens are all over it, and it is not safe. Stay away from Meridian. Repeat, stay away from Meridian—

RACHEL: Fuck. It's automated.

MIRANDA: Still. Haven't heard that one before.

RACHEL: Where the hell is Meridian?

MIRANDA: Far away, seems like.

RACHEL: So he did do it.

MIRANDA: Seems that way.

RACHEL: Damn. *(She finds a free frequency and grabs the ham mic.)* This is—uh… *(She lets go of the mic, looks at* MIRANDA.*)* Do I use his callsign?

MIRANDA: I don't think it matters anymore.

RACHEL: Feels weird to use my name.

MIRANDA: Just pick something.

(Pause. RACHEL *turns back to the mic.)*

RACHEL: This is, uh. Badger. Just north of Pittsburgh, Pennsylvania. We just got a new repeater. Does anybody read?

MIRANDA: Badger?

RACHEL: It was the first thing that popped into my head.

MIRANDA: A bit unorthodox.

*(*RACHEL *makes a face at her. Switches frequencies, and tries again.)*

RACHEL: This is Badger, just north of Pittsburgh. We just got a new repeater. Does anybody read? *(A pause. Static. She switches again.)* This is Badger. We just got a new repeater. Does anybody read? *(Pause. Static. She switches again.)* This is Badger. We just got a new repeater. Does anybody read?

(Pause)

MIRANDA: How long are you planning to do this for?

RACHEL: Until someone answers.

MIRANDA: Great.

\

Scene 11

(A few hours later. Both RACHEL *and* MIRANDA *are in the same places.)*

RACHEL: This is Badger. Anyone read? *(Pause. She switches frequencies.)* This is Badger. Anyone read? *(Pause. She switches frequencies.)* This is Badger. Anyone—

*(*RACHEL*'s voice catches and she coughs.* MIRANDA *gets up, bringing* RACHEL *a water bottle.)*

MIRANDA: Drink. You're going to lose your voice.

RACHEL: I'm a DJ. I'd never lose my voice.

MIRANDA: Drink.

(Grudgingly, RACHEL *does.)*

MIRANDA: You've been at this for hours. How much longer are you going to go?

RACHEL: I told you. Until someone answers.

MIRANDA: You must've been through all the frequencies by now.

RACHEL: So I'll make another pass.

MIRANDA: Rachel.

RACHEL: Clark died for this. Or, best case scenario, got captured for it. I can't let that be for nothing.

MIRANDA: That's not something you can control.

RACHEL: I'm not giving up yet.

MIRANDA: You never did know a losing battle when you saw one.

RACHEL: And you were always too quick to give up.

MIRANDA: Just because I didn't want to end up a night shift DJ in some nowhere little town—

RACHEL: Wow. Because your fancy fucking journalist credentials are doing you so much good at the end of the world, huh? Stranding you halfway across the country with your failure of a friend?

MIRANDA: That's not what I said.

RACHEL: It might as well have been.

MIRANDA: Me leaving wasn't about you. It was about me. What I needed to do for myself, to feel like I had a future. Alright? And it may not be doing me much good now, but it still mattered.

RACHEL: So does this.

MIRANDA: Do you really think you're accomplishing anything here? No bullshit.

RACHEL: I don't know. But I might be.

MIRANDA: You might be.
Rachel, we haven't seen anyone else in *weeks*. Everyone is gone. There is. No. One. Left. Are you ever going to accept that?

RACHEL: Just because we haven't seen them doesn't mean they're not there.

(A long moment)

MIRANDA: I'm leaving.

RACHEL: We can't.

MIRANDA: I am.
I want you to come with me. I want you to let go of this...whatever it is you think you're doing at this point. I don't want to leave you here alone. But I can't keep doing this. I can't just sit here and watch you run yourself into the ground until our luck finally runs out.

RACHEL: Then help me.

MIRANDA: There's nothing I can do to help you. I've tried every way I know to convince you to leave, and you haven't heard a word of it.

RACHEL: I have.

MIRANDA: You haven't. You're too fucking scared to listen.

RACHEL: You said that before. Scared of what?

MIRANDA: To go out. To face what's really happening out there.

RACHEL: That's not…I'm just not willing to give up. Clark, Red, Gwen, even the radio folks, they're all gone. We're the only ones left to keep this going.

MIRANDA: We're the only ones left at all. If you'd been outside, you'd know that.

RACHEL: We just went out.

MIRANDA: To look for Clark. And as soon as we lost his trail, you wanted to come right back.
I know it's hard to face the facts. But you're going to have to, sooner or later.

RACHEL: We can't give up. Or I guess—I can't.

MIRANDA: Fine. But I can't keep having the same argument with you day after day. I have to go.

(Pause)

RACHEL: When?

MIRANDA: Now. Tonight. While it's dark.

RACHEL: Okay.

MIRANDA: Come with me, Rachel. Please.

RACHEL: This can't have all been for nothing.

*(*RACHEL *turns back to the ham station.* MIRANDA *sighs.* RACHEL *continues to repeat the message, frequency after frequency, while* MIRANDA *grabs a bag that is mostly*

already packed and adds a few more supplies to it. It only takes her a minute or two, then she hefts the bag onto her shoulders.)

RACHEL: Guess when you said "now", you meant it.

MIRANDA: I'm tired of delaying the inevitable.

RACHEL: Take a walkie? Just in case.

MIRANDA: What for?

RACHEL: Just in case.

(After a moment, MIRANDA *accepts a walkie, putting it into her bag.)*

MIRANDA: Good luck. I hope someone answers.

RACHEL: Thanks. I hope you find Jess.

(MIRANDA *exits.)*

Scene 12

*(*RACHEL, *alone onstage. Time in this scene should feel slippery, as the isolation and lack of response sink in. The rise and fall of the static should be constant and unrelenting. The lights are dimmer than ever.)*

RACHEL: *(Into the station mic)* This is Rachel. 103.7 WCRP. Hopefully you know that by now, if you've been listening this long, but old habits die hard, eh? I don't have much to offer. We've installed a repeater for our ham setup, but we're…I'm still not picking anyone up. I'm going to keep trying, though. And in the meantime, I'll be here. *(She turns away from the station mic, back to the ham setup, and begins methodically working through the frequencies.)* This is Badger. Does anyone read? *(Click)* This is Badger. Does anyone read? *(Click)* This is Badger. Does anyone read? *(Click)* This is Badger. Please. Does anyone read?

(Time passes. We see RACHEL *pacing the room. Then, back at the station mic.)*

RACHEL: You cannot give up. I don't care how hopeless it seems out there, or how powerful they are. We always have a choice, and you have to choose to keep going. To keep fighting. To stay alive.

(Time passes. RACHEL, *pacing, stopping at the ham mic every couple of laps. Let things get weird here, as* RACHEL *starts to lose her grip on time. Maybe we hear her voice, echoing in the soundscape. Maybe we hear others—maybe recognizable, maybe not. If so, it should be clear that they are imagined.)*

RACHEL: This is Badger. Does anyone read? *(She paces a moment, waiting for a response. Clicks to a new frequency.)* This is Badger. Does anyone read? *(Again)* This is Badger. Does anyone read?

(More time passes. Again at the station mic:)

RACHEL: I know it's hard. I know it might feel like this is never going to end. I know it feels like we've already lost. You have to keep going. You have to.

(Time passes. RACHEL, *passed out on the desk at the ham radio setup. She wakes with a start at some imagined change in the static. Listens intently. There's nothing—just the endless rise and fall. She scrubs at her eyes. Sits for a long moment in silence. Then, suddenly, she jumps up and in a fit of frustration, destroys something—sweeps a shelf, knocks over her chair, whatever is available. The sound crescendos, becoming overwhelming.)*

*(*RACHEL *crosses to the door, throwing it open. She stands for a moment, breathing heavily. She can't bring herself to leave. She crosses back to the table and leans in, pulling both mics to her.)*

RACHEL: This is Badger. You know, there's something I've been wondering about. This whole damn time.

The Legion took out the cell towers. They took out the wifi. I'm sure they crashed satellites. They cut off every mode of talking to one another we had…except this one. Why? Is it just too low-tech for them to bother? Do they not know, somehow? Or are they listening in, right now?
Let's test it. Shall we? If you're listening, you alien fucks, I'll tell you exactly where to find me. Cranberry Township, Pennsylvania. That probably doesn't ring a bell, so let me help you out a little: Pittsburgh. One of the cities you bombed into rubble. Just about twenty miles north. Look for a little red brick building tucked into the side of a hill with a little tower sticking off the top. I'll be waiting for you. Let's finish this.

(Time passes. A long time. We see RACHEL *at the ham mic. We see her pace. We see her sit, staring at the open door, waiting. Eventually, we see her sleep.)*

Scene 13

*(*RACHEL*, alone. Not broadcasting, just listening to the static. The room is even more of a mess than it's ever been. Her food stock is dwindling. The door hangs open. A moment)*

*(*GWEN *steps into view at the door. She's dressed differently, in practical, well-mended clothes. She takes in* RACHEL*, the messy, empty room. Then, she raises a hand, knocking on the door frame in the old pattern.* RACHEL *turns.)*

GWEN: Hey.

RACHEL: Holy shit.

GWEN: I don't know whether to take that as a compliment or not.
Mind if I…?

RACHEL: Yeah. Sure, of course.

*(*GWEN *enters. After a moment, she closes the door behind her.)*

GWEN: Don't worry, I covered my tracks. I promise.

RACHEL: I don't—what happened? Where have you been?

GWEN: It's a long story.

RACHEL: We've got nothing but time.

GWEN: When I left, I went east. That's where it seemed like the most Legion activity was. There's definitely something big going on in Scranton—they're everywhere up that way. The night before I figured I'd reach them, I holed up in a house outside a little town—Trout Run, it was called. Woke up in the middle of the night to a noise downstairs and figured, hey, at least I wouldn't have to walk anymore. So I go downstairs.

RACHEL: It wasn't aliens.

GWEN: No. It was *people.* Humans. I think they were as shocked as I was. Then I just started crying. Bawling my eyes out, snot running down my face, the whole nine. I was so happy to see that we weren't the only ones left that I mean, I couldn't go the Legion anymore. I ended up going back with them. Apparently I just have the kind of face that makes people want to bring me home. There were maybe a dozen of them, holed up in one of the hunting preserves around there, living off the game they could hunt. And they had a radio.

RACHEL: What?

GWEN: A radio.

RACHEL: Could they…?

GWEN: Hear you? No. It's too far. But they could hear others, further east, and up north. When I left, they were gathering supplies, going to try to reach out over

the ham radio, but they've got a ways to go yet. I told them about the alien we killed. How we think they track by smell. Lucky the hunters had been covering their scent from the deer already. I was going to try and come back sooner, give you the good news, but the weather was so bad...
You okay? You look like you're going to pass out.

RACHEL: I might.

GWEN: Please don't. I don't have nearly the first aid knowledge Miranda has. Where is she?

RACHEL: She's gone. Clark, too.

GWEN: Oh. What happened?

RACHEL: Clark disappeared. Miranda...left.

GWEN: Finally went to the military base, huh?

RACHEL: Yeah.

GWEN: Hope she made it okay.

RACHEL: Yeah, me too. She made it a little ways, at least—I heard from her, right before she went out of range.

GWEN: When was that?

RACHEL: I don't know. Weeks ago. Maybe even months.

GWEN: When was the last time you went outside?

RACHEL: It's uh. It's been a while.
They really couldn't hear me?

GWEN: No.

RACHEL: So...have I been talking to anyone at all?

GWEN: I don't know.

RACHEL: Miranda was right.

GWEN: About some things, yeah, I think she was. Listen. I don't know if there's anyone listening or not.

But we met because Miranda and Red went looking, right? And I met the hunters because I went—not looking, necessarily but *out*.

(RACHEL *looks at the mic.)*

RACHEL: This isn't enough.

GWEN: To help people? No. It's a good start—or it was, in the beginning. But it's not enough.

(Pause. The ham radio crackles.)

KV5EDF: This is Kilo Victor Five Echo Delta Foxtrot. Anybody out there receiving?

(RACHEL *grabs the mic.)*

RACHEL: Yes! Yes, we hear you.

KV5EDF: Fuck me sideways. Who am I talking to?

RACHEL: Uh. I guess you can call me Badger.

KV5EDF: Kind of a weird callsign.

RACHEL: I get that a lot?

KV5EDF: Well, in that case, I suppose you can call me Foxtrot. Or Fox, if you prefer. That's what I used to go by locally. And weird callsign or not, I can't tell you how happy I am to hear a friendly voice.

RACHEL: Same here.

KV5EDF: We've got a group together working on getting a repeater network set up down here, see how many people are still out there. Where are you at?

RACHEL: Pennsylvania. You?

KV5EDF: Arkansas. How are things looking up there?

RACHEL: Apocalyptic, if I'm being honest. You?

KV5EDF: I'd say the same. We're hanging in there, though.

RACHEL: Yeah, us too.

KV5EDF: "Us", huh? So there's more than one of you?

RACHEL: Barely, but yes.

GWEN: Hello!

KV5EDF: Don't suppose you've got a weird callsign, too?

GWEN: I'm taking suggestions, I guess?

(Pause)

RACHEL: Fox? You still there?

KV5EDF: I'm here. I just…
We were starting to think we were the only ones left.

RACHEL: Yeah. I know the feeling.

KV5EDF: I bet you do.
Shit—I gotta go. 73, Badger. We'll talk again soon.

RACHEL: Count on it, Fox. 73.

GWEN: "Badger", huh?

RACHEL: It just kind of happened.

GWEN: I like it. It suits you.

RACHEL: Guess I'd better stick with it, then.

GWEN: Hey. Someone heard you.

RACHEL: They did.
But only because of Clark. What he did, getting the repeater working.

GWEN: Right. Sounds like there's a lot more to do where that came from.

RACHEL: Right. *(She checks the time.)* This is normally when I'd do the morning update.

GWEN: Don't let me stop you.

RACHEL: No, I mean…I don't know about you, but I'm getting a little tired of doing this whole alien apocalypse thing alone. If people *are* out there, we should go find them. Right?

GWEN: Sure.
How do we do that?

RACHEL: I dunno. Go out and look? Leave some clues? Light a smoke signal?

GWEN: Um.

RACHEL: That was a joke.

GWEN: Right, right.

(Pause)

RACHEL: Why'd you come back? Not that I'm not happy to see you, but. It's a long way.

GWEN: I guess…you and the others found me when I thought I was the only one left. It felt important to tell you that you weren't alone, either.

RACHEL: Thanks.
Do you think we'll find anyone? Near here, I mean.

GWEN: I hope so.

RACHEL: Me, too.

(A moment)

GWEN: Come outside. The snow is melting.

(After a moment, they exit, leaving the stage empty. The radio static rises and falls.)

END OF PLAY

Made in United States
Troutdale, OR
07/10/2024

21141158R00056